CHILDREN'S PERCEPTIONS OF ELDERLY PERSONS

By Lillian A. Phenice

CENTURY TWENTY ONE PUBLISHING

PUBLISHED BY

CENTURY TWENTY ONE PUBLISHING
POST OFFICE BOX 8
SARATOGA, CALIFORNIA 95070

LIBRARY OF CONGRESS CARD CATALOG NUMBER

80-65604

I.S.B.N.

0-86548-054-0

9.03

TABLE OF CONTENTS

LIST OF TABLES

LIST OF FIGURES

CHAPTER 1

INTRODUCTION

Statement of the Problem

Almost three out of four older people in the United States have at least one living grandchild. Of those having grandchildren, four out of five have seen a grandchild during the past week; more than half have seen a grandchild in the last twenty-four hours (Cottrell, 1974). Cottrell (1974) suggests that when grandchildren are small, there is a good deal of satisfaction in playing the role of grandparent. As the grandparent ages, less satisfaction is involved. However, not much else is known about the reciprocal relationships between the younger and older generations.

The boundaries are not well marked in studying the "old," but as is true of many of the words we commonly use, the adjectives and nouns mean a great many different things to different people. Perceptions of the aged are, then, varied and no generalization should be accepted without knowing who said what about whom. It is important to recognize that much depends upon the one making the assessment. Young children may perceive older people differently than do adolescents or adults. An investigation in the area of children's perceptions of elderly persons can provide researchers with insights into the nature of intergenerational reciprocities.

A recent study by Jantz, Seefeldt, Galper, and Serock (1976) showed that children's attitudes toward the elderly are stereotyped and complex. Frequently, the children rejected the elderly on the basis of physical and behavioral stereotypes. Children viewed the elderly as a group of wrinkled, sad, helpless, funny looking, and passive people who are unable to care for themselves. Jantz et al. concluded that children did not perceive growing old as positive. The children in their study also had only limited knowledge and contact with older persons.

Other research further documents children's negative and stereotyped attitudes toward the aging and the elderly. A study by Treybig (1974) of young children ages three, four, and five years concluded that young children have negative attitudes toward the elderly. Hickey and Kalish (1968) found that as children increased in ages, their image of adult age

1

did not become less unpleasant, but rather stayed the same. Tuckman and Lorge (1965) found that juniors and seniors in high school held common stereotypes and misconceptions of the elderly as being inactive and with complete loss of adult roles. Another study by Kastenbaum and Durke (1964) on adolescents' attitudes toward the elderly showed that old age appeared unpleasant, risky, and without much significant positive value. McTavish (1971) conducted an extensive review of research on attitudes toward the elderly and concluded that there is an overall prejudice towards old people and that the prospect of aging produces negative attitudes. Only one of the three hundred studies examined by McTavish was concerned with children under the age of eleven. Little has been done in this area.

According to Allport (1935) and Klausmeier (1971), attitudes gained in the early years remain as stable enduring influences throughout one's life span. Stereotyped attitudes that children develop may be a strong influence predisposing the individual to act and react in a consistent way, favorable or unfavorable, toward persons, objects, situations, or ideas (Mussen, 1969). It then follows that the perceptions children hold may have a strong influence for interpreting the world and formulating appropriate responses. These perceptions are indications of negative attitudes by members of our young population and they may have far-reaching implications. Children need to develop positive and realistic attitudes toward the elderly in order to be able to develop positive reciprocal interpersonal relations. A society that holds a positive and realisitc attitude towards the aging process and the elderly can only gain in making society a better place for all. A society made up of positive intergenerational contact, aspirations, and motivation become a more fitting place for human development.

Need for the Study

A primary need for this study is to shed light on several aspects of the problem of social perception. How is social perception in children influenced and formed? Data about children's perception of the elderly, whether affected by direct contact with elderly persons or indirect association through books, television, or other informational resources, assist in the investigation of theoretical issues of how perceptions are formed in preschool children during a transitional stage in cognitive and social development.

Much research has emphasized the significance of the family in early life. Parent-child and sibling experiences not only mold behavior but also affect the self-image that becomes vital in later years. Socialization, the process of learning what is expected of an individual, continues long after childhood. Therefore, the nature of the family in which socialization takes place provides a means to understanding what is likely to happen. Since family influences are continuous, one could choose any point as the beginning from the moment of birth of a child or to entrance in public schools. The very great emphasis that child psychologists and social workers have placed on the significance of parental attitude and behavior has forced many people to blame themselves for all the shortcomings of their children. But the fact remains that the child is greatly influenced also by other factors such as heredity, peers, mass media, and by the unavoidable consequences of events over which the parents have no more control than do the children. This is often overlooked, both in literature and by the parents themselves. Therefore, rather than assume that family members are the only primary significant inputs it is necessary to look at other factors that may be contributing to children's perceptions of the elderly. The child's interaction with others is only a part of a world or social order perceived by the child when relating to others, objects, or situations. There is a need for establishing the relationship between significant inputs and children's perceptions.

Another problem needing further study is the social action concern for the loss of potential human resources due to negative stereotyping attitudes concerning the elderly. Although economic, political, educational, and equal opportunity are espoused axioms of American democracy, the elderly are often not accorded this sense of security. Throughout the world one of the basic interests of the aged is to remain as active participants in personal and group affairs (Slater, 1963). Data also appear to be limited on how children perceive the elderly; however, there is limited evidence that shows children hold negative perceptions of elderly persons.

Another need which cannot be revealed in measures of immediate impact but of vital concern is the development of a child's awareness. As the child develops physically, the child should also grow in his ability to understand the feelings of others. In order to gain a sensitivity to and concern for the needs of others, the child must begin learning at an early age.

Objectives

The objective of this research is to answer basic questions regarding children's perceptions of elderly persons by using two methodological procedures of analyses, a descriptive discussion as well as objective instrumentation. Preschool children enroll in the Foster Grandparent Day Care Program in Lansing, Michigan will be compared with preschool children enrolled in regular day care facilities that do not have elderly volunteers or aides present. Specifically, answers to the following questions will be sought.

1. Is there a difference in perception of the aging and elderly between the preschool children in a Foster Grandparent Program and a comparison group comprised of preschool children in a regular day care setting?

2. Do the two groups of children express differences in attitudes about growing old themselves?

3. Is there a relationship between the children's perceptions of the elderly and the children's perceptions of grandparents?

4. Is there a difference between children's perception of the elderly and parental attitudes about the elderly?

5. Which environmental factors are related to children's perceptions of the elderly?

Hypotheses

The following hypotheses will be tested:

Hypothesis 1:
Preschool children enrolled in a Foster Grandparent Day Care Program (Group A) will evidence a difference in perceptions of the aging and the elderly than the preschool children in regular day care facilities (Group B).

Hypothesis 2:
Preschool children in a Foster Grandparent Day Care Program (Group A) will evidence a greater variety of perceptions toward the aging and the elderly than the preschool children in regular day care facilities (Group B).

Hypothesis 3:
Preschool children in a Foster Grandparent Day Care Program (Group A) will evidence a greater amount of direct contact with the aging and the elderly than Group B.

Hypothesis 4:
Preschool children in Group A will evidence more positive
feelings about getting old themselves than Group B.

Hypothesis 5:
Children's perceptions of grandparents will show a relationship with children's perception of elderly persons.

Hypothesis 6:
Children's perceptual responses about elderly persons will
show a difference from parents' responses about the elderly.

Hypothesis 7:
Children who spend more time with grandparents have a more
positive perception of grandparents than those who spend less
time with grandparents.

Hypothesis 8:
Children who spend more time with grandparents have a more
positive perception of elderly persons than those who spend
less time with grandparents.

Assumptions

The following assumptions underlie this study:
1. The preschool years are critical to the child's
development of social cognition and are unique for each child.
2. The parents' previous experiences and the way they
view the elderly play a role in their family interaction and
parent role.
3. The child's experiences in the near environment
affect the child's perceptual responses concerning the elderly.
4. The interview design is an appropriate method for
collecting information from preschool children.
5. The questionnaire form is an appropriate method for
collecting information from an adult family member about the
child's home and family environment.

Limitations of the Study

This study is limited to the children and parents who
participated in day care units in Lansing, Michigan and,
therefore, generalizability is not appropriate. In an
attempt to equate the groups, Group B was roughly compared
to Group A on pertinent variables such as age, sex, type of

day care program, and geographic proximity. However, differences of other experiential variables do exist. In this ex post facto research, one cannot manipulate or assign subjects because the independent variable or variables such as the experiential variables have already occurred (Kerlinger, 1973).

The validation procedures of the study are limited in that only one validated instrument was available to obtain the necessary information from the children. There are severe limitations imposed in reporting the data obtained from the use of the CATE Instrument. The data obtained from the open-ended questions in the Word Association Subtest are objectified into restricted categories and coded so that much interpretive data are lost. This researcher incorporates two methodological procedures for coding the data, an objective quantification as well as the subjective interpretation of the results. The inclusion of both types of coding procedures is based upon the nature of the topic; perceptions are highly interpretive and much information is lost when we quantify the answers completely.

The parental questionnaire was specifically designed for this population. Lack of available funds precluded any attempts to obtain a larger sample.

This study is also limited in that there has not been extensive recent research regarding preschool children's perceptions of elderly persons. In the studies that have been previously conducted, no definition as to what was considered elderly was made to standardize the results. This resulted in a clouded picture of just who and what the elderly represented to the preschool child.

Conceptual Definitions

The following terms are used throughout this study.

CATE. - The CATE is an instrument called Children's Attitudes Toward the Elderly developed and validated by Jantz, Seefeldt, Galper, and Serock (1976) at the University of Maryland. This test was designed to assess children's attitudes toward old people through analysis of the affective, behavioral, and knowledge component of attitudes.

Elderly. - In some capacities age is thought to be the indicator; in others social-psychological factors or physiological changes are used for assessments. According to Webster's New Collegiate Dictionary, it refers to someone somewhat old and advanced beyond the middle age. Cottrell (1974) suggests that much depends upon the person making

6

the assessment. For the purpose of this study, the elderly
will be viewed in relation to Cottrell's definition which is
the definition of the person making the assessment.

Family. - The family is defined conceptually as two or
more interacting individuals who share living space and some
common resources and have a commitment to each other over
some time.

Grandparent. - A parent's parent; an ancestor in the
next degree who is above father or mother in lineal ascent.

Human resources. - Human resources are abilities and
characteristics of the individual along with other resources
which cannot be utilized independently of the individual.
Specific human resources include time, abilities, skills, and
attitudes (Wetters, 1967).

Learning. - Learning is the acquisition of new behavior
as a result of experience (Pickering, 1969).

Perception. - Perception is the process of knowing
objects, facts, or truths, whether by sense, experience, or
by thought; awareness of objects.

Significant inputs. - In this study significant inputs
will refer to "significant others" as well as information.

Conceptual Orientation

One may define socialization as the process by which
someone learns the ways of a given society or social group
so that he can function in it. This includes learning and
internalizing appropriate patterns, values, and feelings.
Since the socialization process occurs through social relationships, a child cannot learn the ways of the society by
being apart from people; others, wittingly or unwittingly,
teach the child through their guidance, examples, responses,
and emotional attachments. Thus, socialization is a function
of social interactions (Elkin, 1960).

There is no one theory that has received general accep-
tance in the area of social cognition. However, in this
study, the social learning approach by Bandura (1977) will
provide the theoretical foundation necessary within a social
psychological approach. It is recognized that a child is
born in an on-going society with common symbols, established
patterns, and recognized positions; and it is through others
that a child learns these elements of the social world. The
behavior of "significant others" and the process of learning,
incidental as well as by direct training, become crucial
elements in explaining the socialization process (Bandura

7

and Huston, 1967).

However, the socialization approach is not adequate by itself in describing the multifaceted phenomenon of human development. The interplay of various environments makes it necessary to view the child in a dynamic ecosystem. For example, underlying the social development of the child is the biological factor. The biological organism requires a suitable input from its near environment such as food, warmth, space, air; it then follows a systematic and orderly pattern in the development of neural, muscular, and glandular tissues. No amount of training can enable a person to function in a given way before he is biologically ready. Maturation and socialization are highly interrelated. Swiss psychologist, Jean Piaget (1896), noted for his work with nursery school children, showed that there are distinct lines of development and that quite early in a child's life social factors combine with physiological development to influence the child's ways of thought and perception of the world.

The agencies of socialization such as the family, community, the school, the peer group, media, and mass communication create a flow of informational input and output resulting in mechanisms for interactions between the social as well as the technological and physical environments. The degree to which a child's ecosystem is open or closed to the family ecosystem depends upon the relationship between the adult and the child. If the parent's perception of elderly persons is positive and realistic, then the system will remain open to the child and will affect the child's perceptions. The child will have a more positive and realistic perception of elderly persons. If, on the other hand, parents hold negative attitudes concerning the elderly, the family may partially close its boundaries in the area of intergenerational reciprocities as well as in controlling and defining the parameters of the child's ecosystem thereby allowing for a more negative stereotype input as found in the general population.

Overview

Chapter II includes a survey of current literature as it applies to children's perceptions of persons. The selection of the sample as well as a description of the instruments and the procedures used for collecting and analyzing the data are discussed in Chapter III. A description and discussion of the subjects and their environments are found in Chapter IV. An analysis and discussion of the data and results of the study are presented in Chapter V. Summary, conclusions, and recommendations for further research are explicated in Chapter VI.

CHAPTER 2

REVIEW OF THE LITERATURE

The literature important to this study is reviewed under the following general headings: the development of social cognition, social psychological theory of person perception, and research related to children's attitudes toward the elderly.

Social cognition of adults, but not children, has been empirically studied throughout this century; however, in the area of person perception, little research has been conducted. Only in the last decade has there been research in the area of the development of person perception. In the recent past social behavior was studied largely from the perspective of psychoanalytic theory or social learning theory (Shantz, 1975). According to Flapan (1968) and Livesley and Bromley (1973), most of the recent studies are not based on any one theory but incorporate social learning theory as well as theory concerning cognitive development.

The Development of Social Cognition

From birth onward the individual lives and develops in a social context that determines much of what may appear to be matters of choice. How the child is reared, what is eaten, the language spoken, and the nature of the child's interpersonal relationships are all reflected in a range of possibilities presented by the culture. The concept culture is an abstraction employed by the anthropologists. The anthropologists use the concept to attempt to comprehend (make sense of) the relationship between individuals and the settings in which behaviors occur. According to Kluckhohn (1954) the existence of culture is inferred on the basis of the observed regularities in the behavior of specific individuals and from the multitude of cultural artifacts that derive from the behavior. Culture, in this sense, is defined in terms of its external, directly observable effects. Prohnasky (1965) suggested that in order to explain these effects or observed regularities of behavior, anthropologists must also assume the existence of an inner culture, the internalized representations of these behavior patterns in the form of norms, attitudes, beliefs, values, and needs.

A substantial repertoir of manners, folkways, and mores

is transmitted to children in the same way that language and concepts are, namely by listening and watching others and by repetitive demonstrations through children's imitation and role learning. This process is variously described in behavior theory as vicarious learning (Logan, Olmsted, Rosner, Schwartz, and Stevens, 1955), observational learning (Maccoby and Wilson, 1957), and role taking (Sears, Maccoby, and Levin, 1957). Incidental learning appears to be a result of active imitation by the child of attitudes and patterns of behavior that significant others have never directly attempted to teach. According to Bandura and Huston (1967), part of a child's behavior is believed to be acquired through identification with important adults in the child's life.

During the socialization process a child uses a range of situational cues, those that the parents may consider immediately relevant and proceed to teach the child and other cues of behavior which the child observes and learns even though instruction to do so has not occurred. The use of incidental cues by both human and animal subjects are well documented by research (Esterbrook, 1959). These cues help to form conceptual formulations that are stored by the child. How much as well as the kinds of conceptual formulations depend usually upon the human and material resources made available to the child. Studies by Hill and Stafford (1971) indicated that children of differing socioeconomic backgrounds enter grade school with very unequal amounts of resources having been invested in them. The data suggested that higher income families actually spend more time and money in socializing their children than families of lesser income. The human and material resources help to provide the social transmissions. Parents, siblings, and all others who regularly impinge on the child present a variety of personal and cultural traits to which a child responds in different ways. Parents, siblings, others, and all informational inputs constitute what is often termed "significant others."

However, this does not mean that the model of a "significant other" acting upon a malleable and unformed child is one proposed in this study for it is an oversimplification. The traditional unidirectional approach of socialization research cannot accommodate complex data as well as provide an impetus for a more complex view of socialization.

Yarrow (1960), in her analysis of children's attitudes and values, made some observations that can be applied to social perception. Substituting perceptions for attitudes and values in the following remarks leads to a conclusion

11

consistent with the present analysis.

> Couplings of parent practices and the behavioral
> outcomes are only in the vicinity of +.25 to +.35
> correlations, attention to intervening conditions,
> among them the child's attitudes and values may
> refine these relationships. What is experienced
> by the child? What is the nature of the cognitive
> framework in which he interprets the parent's
> actions, the nature of the attitudes and values
> brought to play by the parent's behavior?...The
> predictions or explanations of children's behavior
> without regard to the intervening attitudinal or
> value states suffer many errors. Incorporating
> attitudes and behavior into explanatory schemes
> would seem to be a needed elaboration in research
> design and theory, even though resulting formula-
> tions will be less tidy. (Yarrow, 1960, p. 649)

Kephart (1961) in his comprehensive study raised an
important issue related to how the researcher is to interpret the effects of a given parental action on a child; is
the important fact the action itself or the child's perception of that action?
As Hawkes (1957) states:

> It is not sufficient or even realistic to assume
> that, because a mother fondles a child, the child
> sees this attention as a sign that his mother loves
> him. It is not the physical nature of the stimulus
> which determines reaction but rather the way in
> which that stimulus is interpreted by the individual
> stimulated. In each case this will be a highly
> individual interpretation. (p. 47)

Dubin and Dubin (1965) postulate that a child's behaviors and attitudes do not necessarily relate to any particular aspect of the home or early environment. These
behaviors and attitudes seem, rather, to be determined by
the nature of the child and the child's interpretations of
the totality of the experiences in which they occur.
Most reviewers of socialization research have become
sensitized to child-effects. Therefore, any explanation
and interpretation of correlations between "significant
others" does not indicate the direction of effects. In this

particular study these important findings are recognized:

1. The behavior and appearance of the child are a very compelling part of the stimulus field for the "significant other."

2. If the "significant others" are effective, they must, in turn, be affected by the products of their tutelage.

3. Misleading information is obtained if the process of socialization is overlooked and only the final outcome is attended to in the association of child and "significant other" characteristics.

4. The child's characteristics play a role in interactions, i.e., phenomenon such as child battering.

5. Parents do not have a uniform impact on all children in their family and the differences are not merely a matter of sibling birth order and sex role.

6. Effects of the young on parents and adults can be demonstrated experimentally.

This summary is adapted from the work of Bell and Harper, 1977.

What does socialization mean from the child's point of view? It usually consists of being immersed in a continuing sequence of social contexts, family, school, play group, and community in which the child experiences people, objects, rewards, punishments, love, and threats. The child is influenced by people in various culturally determined contexts who are agents of culture. Attitudes, ideals, values, and perceptions are part of the milieu in which the child lives. At home, in the community and at the day care or nursery school, the child has many meaningful experiences. Out of these experiences attitudes, ideals, values, and perceptions are acquired. These learnings take place at all ages but are more pronounced during childhood than during adolescence or adulthood (Garrison and Jones, 1969). Many everyday experiences are important determiners of how the child reacts at different stages of development. According to Allport (1935), attitudes arise out of one's experiences early in life and serve as a basis for the acquisition of later attitudes. The child's early experiences with people will largely determine later attitudes toward people and objects. By the time the child reaches school some measure of favorable and/or unfavorable attitudes towards people and conditions has been acquired. According to Emmerich, Goldman, and Shore (1971) and Sigel, Saltz, and Roskind (1967), the child makes a succession of social judgments of an individual in an ongoing sequence of behavior, often a person with whom the child has interacted before. Ability as well as disposition to recall

13

past events may influence the meaning attributed by the child to the individual's behavior in the current situation. The child may form simple associations or find similarities between the person being judged or interacted with and other friends or acquaintances which would provide added cues for making inferences about the person. Schantz (1975) suggested that the possible perceptual and conceptual processes involved in understanding others involve both the intuitive as well as logical abilities when making social judgments.

Social Psychological Theory of Person Perception

Perceptions help to build concepts. As one perceives qualities, an image, a concept, a meaningful whole is organized and then the senses and feelings are objectified. This objectification provides feedback which serves as further stimulus for modifying percepts and concepts as well as in forming new ones. Associations are influenced by internal as well as external stimuli and are reinforced at intellectual and intuitive levels. As interaction and integration occur, one begins to develop attitudes and values concerning that which is perceived (Gibson, 1969; Merleau-Ponty, 1964; Solley and Murphey, 1960).

According to Shantz (1975) "person perception" is the phrase used by social psychologists in explaining the perceptual and conceptual process involved in understanding others. The earlier person perception studies by Gollin (1958) and Signell (1966) and the more recent studies by Scarlett, Press, and Crockett (1971) were based on Werner's organismic theory. Werner postulates that all development is a process of transition from a global undifferentiated state to states of greater differentiation, specification, and hierarchic integration. The developmental shift is from egocentrism to perspectivism (Langer, 1970).

A primary concern in person perception is the question of how a child describes or categorizes another person or the actions and what dispositions or traits the child attributes to another. According to Piaget (1952) throughout life, beginning in early childhood, people and objects are classified, labeled, and thus categorized. Concerning categorizing Allport (1954) states:

> The human mind must think with the aid of categories. Once formed, categories are the basis for normal prejudgment. We cannot avoid the process.

> Orderly living depends upon it. It is in this
> process that attitudes are learned and thus
> formed. (p. 20)

If, therefore, the social development of children is cognitively based then any description of shape or pattern of a structure of social responses necessarily entails some cognitive dimensions.

The data in studies concerning how children describe other people are divided into two large categories. One such category is labeled overt descriptions which includes aspects of physical appearance, possessions, and family memberships. The other category is labeled covert descriptions which deals with the other persons' abilities, attitudes, and personality traits.

Livesley and Bromley (1973) found in their study of person perception among 320 young people ages seven to fifteen that the number and proportion of psychological descriptions increased insignificantly with age. However, the greatest increase differentiation was observed between the ages of seven to eight years. The seven-year-olds tended to focus on overt qualities like physical appearance and material possessions. Older children used more inferential concepts such as values, beliefs, and disposition. It was found that seven-year-olds used an average of about five different traits in their descriptions and the number doubled for the eight-year-olds. For instance the adjectives used by seven-year-olds tended to be vague and diffused. They also show a strong evaluative component, e.g., bad, nice, good, horrible.

Peevers and Secord (1973) found the same trends in their sample of eighty subjects from kindergarten to college. Another interesting trend was that liked peers elicited other-oriented descriptions (no personal involvement) while disliked peers elicited more egocentric statements (e.g., "he hits me").

Studies have shown that as the ages of the subjects increased both the number of categories and the use of covert categories increased in describing people they actually knew (Gollin, 1958; Scarlett et al., 1971; Yarrow and Campbell, 1963). This tendency for young children to use appearance and possessions to describe others may reflect the tendency to distinguish this individual from other people.

Dickman (1963) and Flapan (1968) conducted studies involving children and films of people whom they did not know. This was carried out to determine how children discriminate, categorize, infer, and explain the behavior observed and how they characterize the people. As before, the younger children reported overt characteristics. The older children increasingly attempted to explain and characterize the people by inferring thoughts, feelings, and intentions of the actors. Explanations also shifted from situational factors to psychological factors with increased ages. Overall, the greatest changes of all kinds occurred between six and nine years of age. The implications from this study in understanding both person perception and role taking such as an observational learning in children is extremely important especially when considering the effects of mass media, such as television programs and advertising.

According to Solley and Murphy (1960) perceptual development is complex, and it appears impossible to interpret perceptual changes in terms of maturation alone, or in terms of learning alone. The most general principle found is that perceptual learning is dependent upon the level of maturation achieved by a child and conversely the full achievement of maturation can be facilitated or inhibited by the occurrence or nonoccurrence of specific learning experiences. "We see 'things' the way we do as adults largely as a resultant of the interaction of nature and nurture within the context of our culture" (Solley and Murphy, 1960, p. 145).

Interrelationships of Person Perception and Cognitive Abilities

Theorists such as Piaget and Erickson suggest that a child who is advanced in understanding what others see is also advanced in comprehending another's thought. For instance at around the age of three, the child's learning is intrusive and vigorous according to Erickson (1959). The child explores the world and learns more about self as well as roles in the family structure. But also at this time, the child begins to develop and become interested in individuals outside the immediate home, although he may display a fear and distrust of strangers.

However, at around age four, egocentricism tends to be replaced by increased social interaction, and the child develops a more sociocentric conception of conditions and objects of the world. "Children now also attach themselves to teachers, and the parents of other children, and they want to watch and imitate people representing occupations which they can grasp such as firemen, policemen, gardeners, garbage men etc." (Erickson, 1968, p. 122). A significant widening

16

radius of people is influencing the individual. This begins with the mother and extends outwards to the larger community. Significant feelings and attitudes are also shown, beginning with a sense of trust in parents leading to a sense of integrity in adulthood. Anderson (1961) suggested that what is demanded by significant people is considered valuable by the child, and what the "significant others" reject is considered bad. The significant people with their pressures, attitudes, demands, and feelings bestow the structure and content.

The child from about four to seven years of age is dominated by assessment of perceptual cues, and much of the child's language and thought depends upon intuition and trial and error, and the child arrives at conclusions often from single cases. According to Klausmeier and Goodwin (1966, p. 233), "preconcepts that are formed are action ridden, imaginative and concrete, rather than schematic and abstract." The young child attends to highly observable, salient, surface cues of people and situations. For instance, the child would often use appearance and possessions of the person to describe and characterize people (Livesley and Bromley, 1973). Likewise the tendency to center attention on a single aspect of "external" stimuli; attention is focused on the ideas and feelings important to the child (Shantz, 1975).

Between four to seven years of age, the child is basically dominated by perceptual cues and sometimes arrives at conclusions about people from single cases. Therefore, it is imperative to have some understanding about the child's attitudes towards the elderly.

The Effects of Age on the Child's Perceptions of Adults

Research findings indicate that age is a significant determinant of degree of realism of perceptions and degree of subtlety of cues children use in their perceptions.

Mott (1954) demonstrated that among four- and five-year-old children, the older more frequently than the younger knew their mother had a first name or that mother was Mrs. _____. Emmerich (1959) concluded that six- to ten-year-olds ascribed power as a characterizing distinction between sex roles more than children four to five years old. Hess and Torney (1962) reported for the age range seven to fifteen years that the younger more frequently than the older children perceived father as boss in the family while older children more frequently said their parents were about equal as family boss. It was found that with increasing age children's

17

perceptions of adults became more realistic, that is, corresponded more accurately with objective characteristics of persons they knew.

Dubin and Dubin (1965) postulated that there is probably some developmental sequence in the formation of perception. First there is the perception of actual behaviors by perceptions of functioning characteristics of role. Later this is followed by a perception of social role as patterned behavior describing a group of people fulfilling a broad social function.

Piaget's extensive research in developmental psychology suggested two ways in which the description and evaluation of other persons might vary with age. He demonstrated that younger children have an egocentric view of the world - people and things are seen in the child's own highly subjective framework. With increasing age, the child develops reciprocity, or the ability to see the other person's point of view.

Peevers and Secord (1973) hypothesized that the use of simple differentiating items and the high level of egocentricity among kindergarten children may well be a necessary stage in getting to know a person. What first emerges in the establishment of relationships in terms of feelings, feelings that are highly egocentric and have little cognitive content. Later these broad, global impressions and feelings are sharpened and more differentiated person perceptual concepts develop.

The fundamental issue in children's perceptions versus adults' perceptions may be between a description of a person and an explanation of why a person is what he appears to be. These two approaches may be necessary for an accurate interpretation of a person and one view may be incomplete without the other (Peevers and Secord, 1973).

Effects of Sex on the Child's Perception of Adults

In the studies by Hawkes, Burchinal, and Gardner (1957), Kohn and Fiedler (1961), and Meltzer (1943), findings suggested that the sex of the child affects perception. It was generally found that girls were more favorably oriented toward all people than were boys. Girls also reported more satisfactory relations with others including their parents. In spite of the fact that girls reported stronger parental control on their behavior and limitation on their personal behavior, girls had stronger positive orientations toward others (Kell and Aldous, 1960). There are no studies

18

permitting analysis of these characteristic differences in perception of adults by boys and girls.

Research Related to Children's Attitudes
Toward the Elderly

An analysis of research literature indicates that in the general population negative attitudes toward the elderly are commonly found. McTavish (1971) in a review of literature and research findings on perceptions of old people found a prevalence of stereotyped views of the elderly. These stereotyped views of the elderly include notions that old people are generally slower, forgetful, less able to learn new things, grouchy, ill, tired, not sexually interested, withdrawn, feeling sorry for themselves, less likely to participate in activities except in religion, unproductive and deficient in various combinations.

The study by Jantz, Seefeldt, Galper, and Serock (1977) showed both negative and positive dimensions. Some of the negative characteristics assigned were sick, ugly, and sad while the positive characteristics assigned were rich, wonderful, and clean. However, when the children reported their knowledge of the elderly in affective terms, their comments tended to be positive; but when reporting in physical descriptive or behavioral terms, their attitudes tended to be negative. The results in this particular study show a mixture of positive feelings of affective dimensions. Jantz et al. (1977) concluded that children did not perceive growing old as positive and expressed negative attitudes associated with aging. Not much was known about the amount of contact these children had with elderly except for the fact that children had few contacts with the elderly outside their own family.

Hickey and Kalish (1968) also found children's negative and stereotyped attitudes toward the aging and the elderly. Tuckman and Lorge (1956) and Kastenbaum and Durkee (1964) found that there was an overall prejudice towards old people and the prospects of aging influenced the formation of negative attitudes in the younger population. The findings of Treybig (1974) indicated that children ages three, four, and five held negative views toward the elderly. These children expressed the concern that they never wanted to get old. However, Thomas and Yamamoto (1975) studied one thousand children in grades six, eight, ten, and twelve and concluded that children did not share the general negative attitude toward old age as found in other studies.

Except for the findings from the study of Thomas and Yamamoto (1975), the prospects of aging are unpleasant and without much significant positive values. Young children's perceptions of the elderly are commonly stereotyped and do not become less unpleasant as they increased in age, but rather stayed the same.

Summary

In this chapter the factors that affect the development of social cognition and especially person perception in children have been reviewed. The child's logical representation of others, how others are characterized and inferences made about their covert and overt characteristics are discussed. The child observes and interacts with people in everyday activities and perhaps the most general finding is that young children especially before the age of seven attend to highly observable, salient surface cues of people and situations. For example, young children often use appearance and possession of persons to describe a person. Other children beyond seven or eight years of age show a substantial change in ways they describe people. More often the description is in terms of values, beliefs, habits, or traits, that is, more abstract descriptions (Livesley and Bromley, 1973). The differences between younger and older children's descriptions of other people may be due to what cues they attend to and how they interpret the cues attended to.

The perceptual and conceptual processes involved in the development of understanding others may be a process of transition from global, undifferentiated states to states of greater differentiation, specification, and integration (Piaget, 1952; Werner, 1948).

Research findings indicating children's perceptions of elderly ultimately showed that younger children below age seven do use surface cues or overt qualities such as appearance and possessions in making social judgments of elderly persons. However, the whys for the appearance of negative perceptions of elderly persons as found by researchers were not answered by the literature review. It could be that descriptive traits such as sick, sad, wrinkled, they have heart attacks are not necessarily negative perception of the elderly but are in fact overt realities for the child of his particular situation and context when he interacts with an elderly person.

20

CHAPTER 3

PROCEDURE

This chapter is comprised of four areas: selection of subjects, selection and description of instruments, design of the study, and data analysis.

Selection of Subjects

The sample is a purposive one selected on the basis of meeting these criteria: child must be enrolled in a day care center at least four hours a day for five times a week for the previous three months; an agreement of parent and child to participate in the study; and the permission and cooperation of day care personnel. The sample consisted of forty-four parent-child dyads. Twenty-two children enrolled in a day care facility with an ongoing foster grandparent program (Group A) and their parents were compared with Group B, composed of twenty-two children randomly selected from day care centers without elderly persons present during operating hours and their parents.

The foster grandparent program is unique among the sixteen children's day care facilities in Lansing, Michigan. Each day, three elderly volunteers participate as supplementary aids in a classroom of approximately twenty children. These same volunteers spend a half a day with the children from Monday through Friday of each week. This foster grandparent project is sponsored by the Catholic Social Services and has been in operation for approximately a year.

Children in Group A were selected from the only day care facility in Lansing, Michigan, which has a foster grandparent program. An attempt was made to eliminate from the sample children who came sporadically or those who were recent to the program. All of the children had been enrolled at the day care center for at least three months. Children whose ages ranged from late three years old to early six year old were included in this study.

Children for the comparison group (Group B) were randomly selected from day care centers in Lansing, Michigan, which met the established criteria. These criteria were: the day care center must be located in a similar geographic area as Group A; the center must have provisions for a sliding scale rate as found in Group A; and the day care center must not have an elderly person as an aide or volunteer during the day. Three centers were randomly selected which met these criteria; however, permission and cooperation were obtained from only two of the centers. Therefore, the third center was eliminated from the study. Thirteen parents of the four- and five-year-olds who were randomly selected for the comparison group (b) were contacted in Center I of Group B. Eleven parents of the four- and five-year-olds who were randomly selected for the comparison group (B) were in Center II.

All parents who participated in this study were personally contacted. The usual practice was to meet them at the day care center when they came to pick their children up. Other parents were contacted by telephone first in order to obtain a verbal consent before sending them the written consent and a parent questionnaire form. All parents who were contacted by telephone willingly responded to participate in this study. Fifty parents were given questionnaires to take home. The total return rate was 88 percent.

The race and sex of the children who participated in this study are shown in Table 3.1. Children classified as white accounted for 79.5 percent of the sample, 18.2 percent as Black, and 2.3 percent reported other.

The ages and relationships of the respondents filling in the parent questionnaire are shown in Table 3.2. Well over half of the respondents were in their twenties, and only one was over forty. None of the parents were under twenty years of age.

TABLE 3.1
RACE AND SEX OF CHILDREN

| | Sex | | |
| | Males (38.6%) | Females (61.4%) | Total |
Race	N	N	N
Black (18.2%)	6	2	8
White (79.5%)	11	24	35
Other (2.3%)	0	1	1
Total	17	27	44

TABLE 3.2

AGES AND RELATIONSHIP OF THE RESPONDENTS FILLING
IN THE PARENT QUESTIONNAIRE

Age	Mother (93.2%) N	Father (6.8%) N	Total N
20 - 24 (15.9%)	7		7
25 - 29 (52.3%)	22	1	23
30 - 34 (18.2%)	7	1	8
35 - 39 (11.4%)	4	1	5
40 - 45 (2.2%)	1		1
Total	41	3	44

Selection and Description of Instruments

In designing this research study, a modified version of CATE, Children's Attitudes Toward the Elderly Instrument by Jantz, Seefeldt, Galper, and Serock, 1977, was decided upon as the assessment instrument for the measurement of the children's perceptions; and a questionnaire designed by the researcher was used for obtaining other data from parents such as demographic, attitudinal, and general information about the child's experiences with elderly persons.

Children's Attitudes Toward the Elderly Instrument (CATE)

Modified versions of three of the four subtests of the CATE were appropriate for the study. The testing time of the CATE is short, approximately fifteen minutes in one session for the preschool child. The first subtest is a word association modification test in which open-ended questions are utilized. The second, a semantic differential, employs standardized bi-polar scales on the evaluative dimensions of attitudes. The third employs concrete visual representations to elicit responses. The utility of a concrete pictorial representation is grounded in the research of child development which indicates that young children have difficulty in handling abstract concepts.

Subtest I - Word Association

The Word Association Subtest is composed of open-ended type questions. This method of assessing children's perception of the elderly has been used by various researchers such as Golde and Kogan (1959) and Treybig (1974). The child's performance on this subtest serves as an indication of the cognitive, affective, behavioral, and physical components of preschool children pertaining to their perceptions of older people. During the testing phase of the Word Association Subtest it became necessary to sometimes substitute other concepts for certain words such as big for very. The children themselves often made the substitution. Since the design is meant to elicit the most information pertaining to children's perceptions of elderly persons, the substitution of appropriate words had little effect on the validity of the instrument.

There are three areas measured in the Word Association Subtest. The first section measures the cognitive component, section 2 measures the affective component, and section 3 measures the behavioral component.

Section 1 - Cognitive Component

To measure the cognitive component of children's perceptions, the following questions are asked: (1) Tell me about old people. (2) What old people do you know? (3) Give me another name for old people.

Responses to question one are scored as belonging to one of three categories within the cognitive component:

(a) <u>Affective</u> - feelings that are expressed such as they are mean, kind, or "I like them."

(b) <u>Physical</u> - pertaining to personal appearance of physical attributes such as "they have wrinkles," gray hair, or "they look pretty."

(c) <u>Behavioral</u> - responses that describe life style characteristics of older people such as the things they do or like "they die," "they walk slow," "they have money." A frequency count is then tabulated for the entire sample giving an indication as to how children view old people in terms of affective, physical, and behavioral ages. In addition, the degree of positiveness or negativeness is measured by rating a specific response as positive, realistic, or negative. Examples of a positive response could include statements such as "they're nice," or "I like them." Negative responses could be "I don't like them," or "they are mean." Realistic responses could be "they have wrinkles," or "gray hair." After each response is given a positive,

24

negative, or realistic rating, a score for each subject is determined by subtracting the number of negative responses from the combined score of the positive and realistic responses. This is done for all subjects across categories.

In the original CATE, each response is given a positive or negative rating and a score for each subject is determined by subtracting the number of negative responses from positive responses. This is done for all subjects across all categories in order to determine if there are differences in degree of positive and negative responses on the basis of the category or whether responses in general are more positive or negative. However, some of the physical characteristics such as "they have wrinkles" or "gray hair" were not considered as being negative by the researcher; and, therefore, another category, a realistic dimension, was added to the rating and the coding of the data.

Responses to questions two and three are coded "yes-no" and analyzed separately to yield a measure for each subject's knowledge of other older persons.

Section 2 - Affective Component

To measure the affective component, children are asked, "How do you feel about getting old?" The children's responses are divided into three categories:

1. Positive - The subject will give some indication that he/she feels good about it.

2. Neutral - The child may give responses that imply one has little control over getting old such as "That's the way it has to be," or "It's okay."

3. Negative - Responses such as "I don't want to," or "bad," or "I'll feel sad" are indications of an aversion to getting old.

Each child is given either a positive, neutral, or negative score for this question. If two answers are given, one negative and one positive, the score would be neutral as they would cancel out each other.

Section 3 - Behavioral Component

To measure the behavioral component, children are asked: (1) What do you do with an old man? (2) What do you do with an old woman? Responses to these questions are divided into three categories for scoring purposes. These categories are:

1. With-active. - Activities indicating joint participation between the subject and the older person.

2. With-passive. - Responses related to quiet activity

25

such as talking or doing something together that is quiet and passive in nature.

3. For. - Here, either the subject or the older person is doing something for the other person. For example, if the older person is seen as "cooking for me," "giving me presents," "goes to the store for him," when the action is on the part of only one of the parties.

Each subject receives a score for the individual categories based on a frequency count.

Validity and reliability. This Word Association Subtest has been administered to a random sample of children (N=180) ages three to eleven. It has been found in the study by Jantz et al. (1976) that children show a consistency of understanding of and response to test items. Coefficients of inter-rater relatively on category scoring ranged from .79 to .98 (Jantz, Seefeldt, Galper, and Serock, 1976).

Administration of the Open-Ended Questions

A few days were spent at each of the day care centers prior to the gathering of data. After establishing rapport with the children, the examiner interviewed each child on a one-to-one basis preferably in a room away from the rest of the children. However, flexibility and adaptability were of prime necessity; for in many instances, the interviews were conducted on the stairs, in hallways, and, if lucky, a special room that was set apart from the rest of the children. Exact wordings were carefully recorded on paper to insure a complete response. If the child did not respond for approximately thirty seconds, the next question was asked.

Subtest II - Semantic Differential

The ten items on the Semantic Differential for this study are the same as found in CATE (1976). Results of their study indicate that this is an appropriate subtest of the evaluation afjectives for young children who indicate a consistent understanding of adjectives and choice possibilities (Jantz et al., 1976).

The bipolar adjectives selected for evaluation are:
1. Good-bad
2. Happy-sad
3. Right-wrong
4. Wonderful-terrible
5. Pretty-ugly
6. Friendly-unfriendly

       7. Clean-dirty
       8. Rich-poor
       9. Healthy-sick
      10. Helpful-harmful
The polarity of the ten item bipolar adjectives scales is
rotated so that half are in one direction and half in the
other.

Validity and Reliability of the Semantic Differential
       Jantz et al. (1977) in their study administered the sub-
test to a random sample of 180 children ages three to eleven
and found a consistent understanding of adjectives and choice
possibilities on the part of younger children. Thomas and
Yamamato (1975) have also supported the applicability of
using a semantic differential technique with young children.
Factor loadings for four of the adjective pairs selected for
use on the CATE were friendly-unfriendly (.92), ugly-pretty
(.83), wrong-right (.80), and bad-good (.93). Factor loadings
for the other six pairs of adjectives were not available.

Administration of the Semantic Differential
       The Semantic Differential is administered orally to the
children by examiners. Each child is asked to rate one concept at a time. For instance, the child is asked, "Are old
people good or bad?" When the child selects one or the other,
he is then further asked the degree of his responses. For
example, if a child responds that old people are good, the
examiner will inquire, "Are they very good or a little good?"
This allows the examiner to place a mark on one of the five-
point scales. The same procedure is used throughout the ten
bipolar items. There is a range of five points on each scale,
and the score for each scale can be one to five. Examples
are:
      Very   A little Don't A little Very
      Good-   good-   Know- bad-   Bad-

      Very   A little Don't A little Very
      Sad   sad   Know   happy   Happy

Subtest III - Concrete Representation
       Since various researchers (Lawrence, 1973; Thomas and
Yamamato, 1975) have successfully used concrete representations such as drawings and photographs as a means of elicit-
ing attitudinal responses from children, the picture on the
cover of the June 1972 issue of the Gerontologist was used

to represent concrete representations of elderly persons (3 males, 3 females). Research findings in child development indicate that young children have difficulty handling abstract verbal concepts (Piaget, 1967). Therefore, the utility of a concrete pictorial representation is grounded in the research on child development.

Section I
Which of these people would you like to be with? Why? The subject was asked to point to an elderly person for the first question. To the second part of the question, why?, three types of responses were scored:
1. Age related - Any response referring to age such as "He looks younger."
2. Altruistic - Responses suggesting having the older person's interest in mind, i.e., "I want to take care of him," "I can cook for him."
3. Evaluative - Responses include comments such as "He looks nice," "He's happy," "He can give me things."

Section II
What kinds of things could you do with that person? Responses were scored into three categories: with active, with passive, and for. These categories are the same as in Subtest I.

Validity and Reliability
Jantz et al. (1977) reported coefficients of inter-rater reliability on category scoring for this subtest ranging from .72 to .98.

Administration
Subtest III was administered individually after the child answered Subtest I and Subtest II. The child was handed the magazine cover and was allowed time to look at the photographs of elderly persons. It was extremely important that the examiner adapted the administration of the subtest to the child's speech and age. Instructions were formulated to correspond to the vocabulary of the children three years of age and older. The child was allowed thirty seconds of wait time before the examiner continued onto the next question.

Parent Questionnaire

Four major kinds of information are provided by the

parent questionnaire. The information includes a demographic profile of the home environment of the child, attitudinal information which gives insight into how the parent feels about elderly persons, characteristics of the child's grandparents, as well as general information on available learning resource materials about elderly persons. The complete questionnaire appears in Appendix A.

The questionnaire was pilot tested using five adults from the East Lansing area. This pilot test was conducted to obtain clarity and understanding of wording and directions by the adults.

Administration

Seventy-five percent of the questionnaires were personally handed out to the parents by the researcher. This was important since it allowed for the parent to ask for more explanation of the study if she/he chose to ask. The rest of the questionnaires were handed out by teachers to the parent as they came to pick up their children. These 25 percent were called on the telephone by the researcher to answer any questions that they might have had. Each parent filled out the questionnaire and returned it within two weeks.

Design of the Study

The design of this study is based on the static-group comparison (Campbell and Stanley, 1963) as shown in Figure 3.1. This design is appropriate for this study because Group A which has experienced X (elderly persons in day care centers) is compared to Group B which has not experienced the aid of elderly persons in day care facilities.

Group A	X _ _	01	n = 22
R			
Group B		02	n = 22
Total			N = 44

Fig. 3.1. A Static Group Comparison Design

There are no formal means of certifying that Group A and Group B would have been equivalent had it not been for the X. Therefore, to eliminate some of the differences between the groups, some control in selection of the centers was implemented, such as the experiential variables. Under the ex post factor analysis, matching on background characteristics is usually ineffective and misleading, especially in instances in which the persons in the experimental group have sought out exposure to X (Campbell and Stanley, 1963). However, in this particular study, because the foster grandparent program has been in effect for less than a year, many of the children who attended the center already did so prior to implementation of the foster grandparent program. There is no evidence that the parents/children in the experimental group chose that center because of the foster grandparent program.

Data Analysis

The data obtained from all subjects on all instruments were coded, key punched on computer cards, and verified with the aid of staff members in the Office of Research Consultation (ORC) at Michigan State University. The computer program used for analyzing the data was the Northwestern University Statistical Package for the Social Sciences (SPSS). The inferential statistical tests used in this study were the Wilcoxen t test, Wilcoxen matched t test, Kendall tau, and Sign Test of the Profile Pattern. The alpha level of significance was set at .05 for decisions about rejection of the hypotheses using inferential statistics.

The statistical procedures used to test the differences in the scores of the two Groups A and B with respect to Hypotheses 1, 2, 3, and 4, and the combined Groups A and B with respect to Hypotheses 5, 7, and 8, with the scores of their parents with respect to Hypothesis 6 and the instruments associated with each of them, are shown in Figure 3.2.

Summary

The population for this study was preschool children enrolled in day care facilities in the Lansing, Michigan district. The sample consisted of forty-four subjects and forty-four parents of the subjects. The ages ranged from late three-year-olds to early six-year-olds from surrounding day care facilities. Subjects in Group A consisted of children enrolled in a foster grandparent program and Group B consisted of randomly selected children from criteria selected day care centers. All children were individually interviewed using a modified version of the CATE, Children's Attitudes Towards the Elderly instrument by Jantz, Seefeldt, Galper, and Serock (1977).

A parent questionnaire was also included to gather information on the child's demographic profile of the home environment, attitudinal information about how the parent felt about elderly persons, and actual experiential behaviors as reported by parents of the child's direct and indirect contact with elderly persons.

The data from the two groups were analyzed to compare the responses of the children enrolled in the facility with the foster grandparent volunteers and the responses of children in day care centers without elderly volunteers to determine if the presence of elderly persons had any influence on the subject's responses.

The data from the responses of Group A and Group B were collapsed and then compared with the appropriate parent responses obtained by means of the parent questionnaires. This comparison was made to determine if the child's responses were in agreement with the parent's responses.

Purpose of Analysis	Data Used in Analysis	Statistics
Principal Analysis		
Description of Subjects and Their Environments:		
Profile of parents, profile of grandparents	Demographic data	Frequency Count
Childrens' direct and in- direct experiences	Experiential data	Frequency Count
Parental attitudes toward elderly	Attitude data	Frequency Count
Test of Hypotheses:		
1 & 2	Scores on semantic differen- tial and word association section 1 and 3	Wilcoxen t-test
3	Experiential data	Wilcoxen t-test
4	Scores on word association section 2	
5	Scores on the semantic dif- ferential	Kendall tau & Sign Pro- file Pattern Test
6	Scores on the semantic dif- ferential	Matched Wilcoxen t-test
7 & 8	Experiential data	Descriptive (Frequency Count/ means)

Fig. 3.2. Methods Used in the Analyses of Data

32

CHAPTER 4

DESCRIPTION AND DISCUSSION OF SUBJECTS AND THEIR ENVIRONMENT

In this chapter, data collected from the respondents of the parent questionnaire are discussed and reported.

The Contextual Conditions of the Children

In attempting to describe the subjects, it is also necessary to discuss some of the factors in the near environment that provides the contextual conditions surrounding the child, such as a profile of the families, a profile of grandparents, the children's experiential behaviors of elderly-child interactions, and the children's parental attitudes toward elderly persons.

Profile of Families

The most striking characteristic of the families was that 50 percent of these children came from two-parent households. There were 36.4 percent single parent households and 13.6 percent decided not to comment on their marital status. The marital status of the respondents of the parent questionnaire are shown in Table 4.1. Most of the respondents were mothers (93.2%).

TABLE 4.1
MARITAL STATUS OF PARENTS

	Group A N	Group B N	Total N
1. Never married (2.3%)	1		1
2. Married (50%)	13	9	22
3. Widowed (2.3%)		1	1
4. Separated (4.5%)	1	1	2
5. Divorced, not remarried (27.3%)	5	7	12
6. Don't know (0.0%)			0
7. No response (13.6%)	2	4	6
Total	22	22	44

A small number of households (9%) have other adults, not parents of the child, living with the family. The three varieties of household composition with other adults included were:

1. Two households had a single adult male living in.
2. One household had four other adult females living in.
3. One household had three adults, one married couple and a single adult male, living in.

With respect to educational levels, the largest category (50%) had at least one to three years of college, technical or business training. At least 29.5% of the respondents had a bachelor's degree. As shown in Table 4.2, only 2.3 percent of the parents had less than a high school diploma.

A majority of the respondents (79.5%) considered themselves fully employed at the time they filled in the parent questionnaire as shown in Table 4.3. The respondents chose as many categories as they saw appropriate to their situation. The other categories which had no responses were eliminated from this table but can be found in Appendix A.

Estimated total family yearly incomes are shown in Table 4.4. The median income levels for these particular families using day care facilities is $11,000-$14,999. The estimated total yearly income ranged from two families in the $3,000-$4,999 level to ten families earning over $20,000. The two families at the 3,000-4,999 level were single parent households. The respondents were employed and also students. All ten families earning over $20,000 were two-parent households.

Profile of Grandparents

In order to have a more complete picture of the factors that may affect the child's perception of elderly persons, data on the living grandparents were collected such as grandparents' ages at last birthday, sex, marital status, health, and time spent with the child either by visits or telephone calls.

Forty-three children (98%) in this study have at least one living grandparent. Eighteen (41%) respondents reported the child having all four grandparents living. Seven children (16%) had more than four grandparents which may indicate a remarriage by a parent. There are more living female grandparents than male grandparents as shown in Table 4.5.

Marital status of the children's grandparents are shown in Table 4.6. Only 5.6 percent of the 142 grandparents were

34

TABLE 4.2
EDUCATIONAL LEVEL OF PARENTS IN GROUP A AND GROUP B

Educational Level	Group A N	Group B N	Total N
1. Less than 8 grades of elementary school	0	0	0
2. 8 grades of elementary school	0	0	0
3. 1-3 years of high school	0	1	1
4. Completed high school and received a diploma or passed high school equivalency exam	4	4	8
5. 1-3 years of college, business school, or technical training	10	12	22
6. College graduate, bachelor's degree	3	2	5
7. Post bachelor's course work	2	0	2
8. Master's degree	2	1	3
9. Post Master's course work	1	2	3
10. PhD, EdD	0	0	0
11. Other professional degree (such as MD, DO, JD, DDS): Please specify_____	0	0	0
Total	22	22	44

separated or divorced whereas in Table 4.1 it was noted that nearly 37 percent of the respondents reported a divorced or separated marital status. Well over half of the grandparents were married (69.7%) and 20.4 percent were widowed.

Approximately twice as many of the first three grand-parents were in good health as shown in Table 4.7. However,

TABLE 4.3
EMPLOYMENT STATUS OF PARENTS

Employment Status	No	Yes
Houseperson (31.8%)	30	14
Student (27.3%)	32	12
Part-time employment (13.6%)	38	6
Full-time employment (79.5%)	9	35

TABLE 4.4
ESTIMATED TOTAL FAMILY YEARLY INCOME

	Group		Total
	A	B	
Income Levels	N	N	N
Under 3,000			0
3,000-4,999	2		2
5,000-6,999	2	2	4
7,000-8,999	2	3	5
9,000-10,999	4	2	6
11,000-14,999	3	4	7
15,000-19,999	4	5	9
Over 20,000	4	6	10
No response	1		1
Total	22	22	44

from Grandparent IV the data show a decrease in their health status from good to fair. Sixty-one percent of the grandparents were rated in good health, 30 percent were rated in fair condition, and 9 percent were rated in poor health.

In the study by Jantz, Galper, and Serock (1977), it was found that children had limited contact with elderly persons. Data about children in this study partially support the findings. Total percentages of time children spent with grandparents are shown in Table 4.8. Out of forty-four children, only one child did not have a grandparent. A majority of the children (86.4%) saw at least one grandparent about once each week. Only 6.8 percent of the children saw their grandparents at least once each day. As more numbers of grandparents were reported by the parents, there were less children involved.

TABLE 4.5
SEX AND TOTAL NUMBER OF LIVING GRANDPARENTS

Number of Living Grandparents	Female (57.7%) N	Male (42.3%) N	Total N
1 (97.7%)	26	17	43
2 (86.4%)	23	15	38
3 (70.5%)	18	13	31
4 (40.9%)	9	9	18
5 (15.9%)	2	5	7
6 (11.4%)	4	1	5
Total	82	60	142

TABLE 4.6
MARITAL STATUS OF CHILD'S GRANDPARENTS

Number of Living Grandparents	No Response	Never Married	Married	Widowed Not Married	Separated	Divorced Not Married
1		1	27	14		1
2		1	32	4		1
3	2		19	6	1	3
4	1	1	13	1	1	1
5			5	2		
6			3	2		
Total	3	3	99	29	2	6

Children's Experiences with Other Elderly Persons

Sometimes preschoolers meet elderly persons outside the home. Data were collected to give us a description of the elderly persons the child may have met or been with over a time period of one week. Also data were collected on the total numbers of hours children spend with these particular individuals. Total number of times children see elderly persons classified by sex and age are shown in Table 4.9.

Data indicate that 25 percent of the children see an elderly female 55-65 years old and 13.6 percent see an elderly male of the same age range about once each day.

TABLE 4.7
HEALTH STATUS OF CHILD'S GRANDPARENTS

	Health Status		
	Good	Fair	Poor
Grandparent	N	N	N
Grandparent I	25	12	6
Grandparent II	26	11	1
Grandparent III	21	88	2
Grandparent IV	11	7	0
Grandparent V	1	3	3
Grandparent VI	3	2	
Total N (142)	87	43	12

TABLE 4.8
TOTAL NUMBER OF TIMES CHILDREN SPEND WITH GRANDPARENTS

Total Time Child Sees Grandparents	Number of Children Per Number of Grandparents					
	1	2	3	4	5	6
About once each day (6.8%)	2	1				
About 3-4 times a week (25.1%)	6	1	1	1	1	1
About once each week (86.4%)	12	13	7	4	1	1
About once or twice each month (81.9%)	12	12	7	4	1	
About 6 times each year (36.2%)	3	2	4	2	3	2
About once a year (70.6%)	7	8	9	5	1	1
Never (15.9%)	1	1	3	2		
No Response (1 child, 2.3%)						1
Total N (44)	43	38	31	18	7	6

Approximately 20 percent of the children see an elderly female person 66-75 years old and only 4.5 percent see an elderly male of the same age range at least once each day. Only 6.8 percent of the children see an elderly female seventy-six years and older and none reported seeing an elderly male of the same age range about once each day. The data indicate that more children see elderly females than elderly males during a day.

Sixty-eight and two-tenths percent of the children see an elderly female 55-65 years old and 61.4 percent of the

TABLE 4.9
TOTAL PERCENTAGES OF TIME CHILDREN SEE ELDERLY PERSONS BY SEX AND AGE

Total Time Child Sees Elderly	Sex and Age					
	55-65 Years Old		66-75 Years Old		76 Years and Older	
	Female %	Male %	Female %	Male %	Female %	Male %
About once each day	25	13.6	20.5	4.5	6.8	
About 3-4 times a week	15.9	20.5	11.4	11.4	4.5	2.3
About once each week	27.3	27.3	11.4	15.9	6.8	6.8
About once or twice each month	13.6	9.1	9.1	11.4	9.1	9.1
About 6 times each year	2.3	6.8	6.8	4.5	6.8	4.5
About once a year	4.5		6.8	6.8	18.2	15.9
Never				4.5	19.1	18.2
No response	11.9	22.7	29.5	36.4	38.6	43.2
Total N = (44)						

children see an elderly male of the same age range at least once a week. There is only a slight difference in terms of contact here. Forty-three and three-tenths percent of the children see an elderly female 66-75 years old and 31.8 percent of the children see an elderly male of the same age range at least once a week.

Only 18.1 percent of the children see an elderly female seventy-six and over and 9.1 percent of the children see an elderly male of the same age range about once each week. These data indicate that children have more contact with elderly females than elderly males. But a closer look at the table shows that there are more "no responses" for the male category than the female. Respondents either were not as aware of elderly males or else there were less elderly males in the child's near environment. According to Johnson and Bursk (1977) in the United State's population, there are approximately 57 percent females and 41 percent males over sixty-five years of age. This fact may help to explain the reason for children having less opportunity for contact with elderly males.

Assessment of Elderly-Child Interaction in Different Settings

An effort was made to analyze the amount of interaction by learning about the environment where contacts are made. Data gathered were sparse and this may be due to the fact that the children spend much of their time at the day care centers under other adult supervision. Frequency count of contacts made as well as hours spent with elderly persons in the particular settings are shown in Tables 4.10 - 4.18.

TABLE 4.10
CONTACT HOURS AND FREQUENCY COUNT OF ELDERLY-CHILD
INTERACTION IN PRESCHOOL/DAY CARE FOR A WEEK

	Frequency									
	0	1	2	3	4	5	6	7	8	9
Number of Children N = 44	Number of Elderly Persons									
	27	7	1	2	2		4		1	
Number of Children N = 44	Number of Hours Spent									
	27	4	1							12

Of the forty-four parent-child dyads, twenty-seven parents (61.4%) reported that their child had no contact with an elderly person over the past week, as shown in Table 4.10. This indicates that five parents (11.4%) were unaware of the foster grandparent day care program which their child participated in. Only nine of the forty-four parents (20.5%) indicated their child had contact with at least three different elderly persons. It appears that parents have very limited knowledge of what happens at the day care centers. For children in Group A (N=22) there were three elderly foster grandparents present every day at the day care unit. Out of sixteen children who had some contact with elderly persons in day care settings, twelve children (25%) had more than nine hours of contact per week. The other five children had less than two hours of contact per week with elderly persons.

Not many children had contact with an elderly person in the library as shown in Table 4.11. Only three children were reported as having had contact with an elderly person for at least an hour over the past week. Ninety-three percent of the children had no contact with an elderly person in a library setting.

Children have only a limited amount of contact with the

40

TABLE 4.11
CONTACT HOURS AND FREQUENCY COUNT OF ELDERLY-CHILD INTERACTION IN LIBRARY FOR A WEEK

	Frequency									
	0	1	2	3	4	5	6	7	8	9
Number of Children N = 44	Number of Elderly Persons									
	41	2	1							
Number of Children N = 44	Number of Contact Hours									
	41	3								

elderly in a church setting as shown in Table 4.12. Two children (4.5%) had contact with eight elderly persons and two children had spent at least three hours a week with the elderly. Only 18.2 percent of the children had contact with the elderly in a church setting. This percentage is slightly higher than what is reported as the attendence rate in church attendance for working class adults. Rubin (1976) found in her study that 10 percent of working class families attend church regularly. If one can assume that children attend church with their parents, these data indicate that there is a higher church attendance rate in this sample than found in the working class in Rubin's study.

TABLE 4.12
CONTACT HOURS AND FREQUENCY COUNT OF ELDERLY-CHILD INTERACTION IN CHURCH FOR A WEEK

	Frequency									
	0	1	2	3	4	5	6	7	8	9
Number of Children N = 44	Number of Elderly Persons									
	36	2	4						2	
Number of Children N = 44	Number of Hours Spent									
	36	6		2						

Almost half of the children were reported to have contact with elderly neighbors (43.2%) as shown in Table 4.13. The range of contact was from ten children having had contact with at least one elderly neighbor a week to one child having had contact with seven elderly neighbors over a week's time. Four children had at least nine hours of contact with elderly neighbors in a week's time. The mean number of hours these nineteen children spent with an elderly neighbor was three hours per week.

Nine of the children have some contact with elderly

TABLE 4.13
CONTACT HOURS AND FREQUENCY COUNT OF ELDERLY-CHILD INTERACTION WITH NEIGHBOR FOR A WEEK

	Frequency									
	0	1	2	3	4	5	6	7	8	9
Number of Children N = 44	Number of Elderly Persons									
	25	10	5	2	1			1		
Number of Children N = 44	Number of Hours Spent									
	25	10	2		1		1	1		4

relatives over a week's time (20.5%) as shown in Table 4.14. Three of the nine children who have some contact with elderly relatives (33.3%) have at least nine or more hours of contact with elderly relatives over a period of a week.

During the past week, children had had very limited contact with medical personnel as shown in Table 4.15. Only 15.9 percent of the children have seen at least two elderly persons in a medical setting.

Only a few children have contact with elderly friends (13.6%) as shown in Table 4.16. The mean number of hours spent by the six children with elderly friends was 1.5 hours per child.

Nine children have some contact with elderly persons in stores or in market places (20.5%) as shown in Table 4.17. One child has at least four hours of contact per week, but the rest of the eight children reported to have less than an hour of contact. Thirty-five of the children (79.5%) have no contact with elderly persons in stores or market places. The problem could be that parents are not aware of elderly persons at these places or parents leave the child at home when the parent goes shopping.

TABLE 4.14
CONTACT HOURS AND FREQUENCY COUNT OF ELDER-CHILD INTERACTION WITH RELATIVES (OTHER THAN GRANDPARENTS) FOR A WEEK

	Frequency									
	0	1	2	3	4	5	6	7	8	9
Number of Children N = 44	Number of Elderly Persons									
	35	4	1	1	2					
Number of Children N = 44	Number of Hours Spent									
	35	6								3

TABLE 4.15
CONTACT HOURS AND FREQUENCY COUNT OF ELDERLY-CHILD INTERACTION WITH MEDICAL PERSONNEL FOR A WEEK

	Frequency									
	0	1	2	3	4	5	6	7	8	9
Number of Children	Number of Elderly Persons									
N = 44	37	5	2							
Number of Children	Number of Hours Spent									
N = 44	37	7								

TABLE 4.16
CONTACT HOURS AND FREQUENCY COUNT OF ELDERLY-CHILD INTERACTION WITH A FRIEND FOR A WEEK

	Frequency									
	0	1	2	3	4	5	6	7	8	9
Number of Children	Number of Elderly Persons									
N = 44	38	5	1							
Number of Children	Number of Hours Spent									
N = 44	38	4	1	1						

TABLE 4.17
CONTACT HOURS AND FREQUENCY COUNT OF ELDERLY-CHILD INTERACTION WITH PEOPLE IN STORES OR MARKET PLACES FOR A WEEK

	Frequency									
	0	1	2	3	4	5	6	7	8	9
Number of Children	Number of Elderly Persons									
N = 44	35	3	4		1	1				
Number of Children	Number of Hours Spent									
N = 44	35	8			1					

Child's Indirect Experiences with Elderly Persons

There are many items in the home that contribute to learning. Media sources such as television, newspapers, magazines, books, records, and cassette tapes may have an influence in learning about elderly people. Therefore, data were collected and designated under media categories to help describe the child's near-by learning environment.

During a week's span 18.2 percent of the children had some indirect exposure to elderly persons through the newspapers and magazines. Nearly 7 percent of the children had some indirect contact with elderly persons through records.

Only one child or 2.3 percent had a cassette tape that exposed the child to some perceptions of the elderly. Nine children, or 20.4 percent of the children, had some indirect exposure to elderly persons through books. The largest source of indirect exposure to elderly persons was the television. Approximately 82 percent of the parents reported that their children were exposed to elderly persons on television. Parents reported a child having seen one show per week to eight shows per week containing portrayals of the elderly.

This set of data on television viewing and portrayals of elderly is to be viewed with caution. According to Project Castle (Simmons, Greenberg, and Atkin, 1977), only 3-4 percent of major characters were old, and extremes of age are rare on television.

Parents' Attitudes Toward Elderly Persons

In addition to the demographic and experiential information, the parent questionnaire contained a section on parental attitudes toward elderly persons and grandparents. Analysis of the data is shown on Table 4.19.

Discussion of Findings on Parental Attitudes

More parents (93.2%) felt that grandparents more than elderly persons expected preschool children to obey them and visit with them. Parents felt that grandparents were not as good examples for preschoolers as elderly in general, and only 50 percent of the parents agreed that parents were to be blamed when preschool children did not respect the elderly person or grandparent. Half of the parents felt that grandparents encouraged preschoolers to behave differently from the way the children were told at home. However, parents did not view grandparents as old fashioned in their views about child care and rearing. But parents felt elderly persons in general were more old fashioned.

More parents (97.7%) felt that preschoolers liked their grandparent, and 72.7 percent of the parents felt that children liked elderly persons. More parents felt that grandparents rather than elderly persons liked the preschooler.

The most important dimensions in which 90 percent or more of the parents agreed with were grandparents liked preschool children and preschool children liked grandparents. Parents also felt that grandparents would like the preschool child to visit with them.

44

TABLE 4.18

TELEVISION SHOWS AND THE PERCENTAGES OF CHILDREN
WHO WATCH THEM

Shows	Percentages (N=38)
Waltons	63.2
Mr. Kangaroo	26.3
Sesame Street	23.7
My Three Sons	18.4
Grizzly Adams	15.8
Mr. Rogers	10.5
I Love Lucy	10.5

<u>Below 10 percent</u>

All in the Family
Amazing Spider Man
Baby I'm Back
Barnaby Jones
Bob Newhart
Brady Bunch
Doris Day Show
Electric Co.
Emergency
Fat Albert
Gilligan's Island
How the West Was Won
The Jeffersons
Laverne and Shirley
Little House on the Praire
Love Boat
Muppets
Saturday Children's Film Festival
Saturday morning cartoons
Specials
Studio C
Walt Disney
Wild Kingdom

NOTE: Four children do not watch any television shows. Two parents reported not knowing what shows their children watched that contained elderly portrayals.

TABLE 4.19
PARENTAL ATTITUDE SURVEY TOWARD ELDERLY PERSONS AND GRAND-
PARENTS   (N=44)

1. Do you think elderly persons/grandparents expect pre-
    school children to obey them?

	Elderly Persons		Grandparents	
	N	%	N	%
Disagree	2	4.5	3	6.8
Unsure	4	9.1	0	--
Agree	37	84.1	41	93.2
No Response	1	2.3	0	--

2. Do most elderly persons/grandparents like quiet preschool
    children better than noisy preschool children?

	Elderly Persons		Grandparents	
	N	%	N	%
Disagree	10	22.7	16	36.4
Unsure	7	15.9	7	15.9
Agree	26	59.1	21	47.7
No Response	1	2.3	0	--

3. Can elderly persons/grandparents who are very friendly
    control preschool children?

	Elderly Persons		Grandparents	
	N	%	N	%
Disagree	3	6.8	3	6.8
Unsure	6	13.6	3	6.8
Agree	34	77.3	38	86.4
No Response	1	2.3	0	--

4. Do you think most elderly persons/grandparents are good
    examples for preschoolers?

	Elderly Persons		Grandparents	
	N	%	N	%
Disagree	1	2.3	2	4.5

Table 4.19 continued...

Unsure	11	25.0	13	29.5
Agree	31	70.5	29	65.9
No Response	1	2.3	0	--

5. Do most elderly persons/grandparents really want pre-schoolers to visit them?

	Elderly Persons		Grandparents	
	N	%	N	%
Disagree	2	4.5	0	--
Unsure	14	31.8	2	4.5
Agree	27	61.4	42	95.5
No Response	1	2.3	0	--

6. Are parents to blame when children do not respect the elderly persons/grandparents?

	Elderly Persons		Grandparents	
	N	%	N	%
Disagree	9	20.5	9	20.5
Unsure	12	27.3	13	29.5
Agree	22	50.0	22	50.
No Response	1	2.3	0	--

7. Do you think most elderly persons/grandparents like preschool children?

	Elderly Persons		Grandparents	
	N	%	N	%
Disagree	1	2.3	0	--
Unsure	7	15.9	1	2.3
Agree	35	79.5	43	97.7
No Response	1	2.3	0	--

Table 4.19 continued...

8. Do you think most preschool children like elderly persons/ grandparents?

	Elderly Persons		Grandparents	
	N	%	N	%
Disagree	0	0	0	0
Unsure	11	25.	1	2.3
Agree	32	72.7	43	97.7
No Response	1	2.3		

9. Do elderly persons/grandparents encourage children to behave differently from the way they are told at home?

	Elderly Persons		Grandparents	
	N	%	N	%
Disagree	9	20.5	22	50.0
Unsure	7	15.9	8	18.2
Agree	27	61.4	14	31.8
No Response	1	2.3		

10. Do you think most elderly persons/grandparents are too old-fashioned in their views about child care and rearing?

	Elderly Persons		Grandparents	
	N	%	N	%
Disagree	8	13.6	27	61.4
Unsure	9	20.5	5	11.4
Agree	28	63.6	12	27.3
No Response	1	2.3		

Parent-Child Interaction Before a Visit

To Grandparents

If parents felt that grandparents would like the preschool children to visit with them, what do parents say to prepare their children for the visit? A hypothetical question was asked of the respondents.

Let us just imagine that _____ is old enough to stay overnight at grandparent's home for the first time. How do you think you would prepare him/her? What would you do or tell him/her?

Nearly half of the forty-four parents applied some positive auto suggestive technique; they told their child to "have a good time" or "you'll have a good time." However, in the same breath they followed that phrase with a series of reminders or subtle commands such as "obey g...," "listen to them," "be good," "go to bed early," "brush your teeth," "don't mess," "be quiet," and "be a big girl." Some parents used a form of bribery; others threaten in order to insure an appropriate behavior from the child. An example was "Don't be bad. Please obey them. If you don't you will get a spanking by me when you get home." A few parents reasoned with their child such as, "Don't play around after you are in bed. Grandpa and Grandma will have to get up to get you settled in bed and you don't want them to get tired. They need the rest." Only one parent reminded her child to show some affection to her grandparents. She told the child to "give Granny a kiss for Mom." Approximately one-fourth of the parents reassured the child that the parent was coming back to pick the child up at a certain time.

To Neighbors

Parents were also asked this question:

Let us just imagine that _____ is about to visit with an elderly neighbor for the afternoon while you run on an errand that will take about 2-3 hours. How do you think you would prepare him/her? What would you do or tell him/her?

A technique used by some of the parents was to try to entice or make the visit to the neighbors as attractive as possible. Children were told that the neighbor was looking forward to the visit, how Mrs. _____ would read to her, or reminding the child of the fun he/she had at the last visit. The most common phrases used by parents to prepare the child were "mind her," "obey her," "be good," "don't get into a mess," or "don't get into trouble." There were less reminders as compared to the visit with grandparents. Nearly half of the parents reassured the child as to the parent's return.

49

Comparison of Visit Preparations

Generally parents were not as specific in their preparation and reminders to their children when they visited with neighbors as when they visited with grandparents. There were more do's and don'ts for the child before a visit with grandparents. Also, there were more threats of punishment or enticement for good behavior like a special treat for being good. And yet, at the same time they were told to have fun nearly twice as often as found when visiting with neighbors.

The child was told to put on his best suit of behavior when visiting with grandparents. The atmosphere between parent and child was more intense in demands. This may be due to the intensity of the reciprocal relationship between the parents and grandparents, whereas the demands were less so between parent and child when the child was to visit with a neighbor. Accordingly, the reciprocal relationship between neighbor and parent is less intense. Therefore, parents may moderate their behavior and place demands upon the children according to the nature of the relationship between the parents and others. Further study is necessary in order to determine if in fact there is a relationship between the intensity of the reciprocity between the "other" and the parents, and the intensity of reciprocity between parent and child when situations demand the interaction between the child and the "other." The strength of the reciprocity between parent and the "other" determines the intensity of demands on the child when interacting with the "other." More is expected from someone you know than from a stranger. However, this could also be the result of a methodological problem because the question for grandparents always came before the question for neighbors. This situation may have precipitated an imbalance and respondents answered the first question more fully than the second question.

Summary

This chapter has been devoted to describing and discussing the subjects and their environments. Analysis of the data revealed that 50 percent of the subjects for this study came from two-parent households. The median range for estimated family yearly income was $11,000-$14,900. Of the forty-four parent respondents, 79.5 percent reported having one to three years of college, business school, technical training, or better.

Forty-three children in the sample had at least one

living grandparent. As the number of living grandparents increased, there were progressively less children with living grandparents. Marriages seemed relatively stable for grandparents as only 5.6 percent were divorced or separated whereas 31.8 percent of the children's parents who answered this particular section were divorced. Grandparents were relatively healthy and a majority of the children (86.4%) saw at least one grandparent about once each week.

The children have more contacts with elderly persons in the neighborhood than in any other setting and least contact with elderly persons at the library. However, more than half the parent respondents marked zero for each of the eight social settings (day care, library, church, neighborhood, relatives, medical, friend, market places) indicating a possibility that parent respondents were not fully aware of the children's experiences during the day.

Parental attitudes toward the grandparents and elderly showed that parents felt grandparents liked preschool children and wanted the children to visit with them. Parents also felt that children liked their grandparents. However, 50 percent of the parents felt that parents were not to be blamed when children did not respect elderly persons or grandparents. It seemed that slightly more parents felt that grandparents were not as good examples for their children as elderly people in general. This presents an interesting phenomenon, as the old saying goes, "The pasture always looks greener on the other side of the fence." This adage also seems to apply when evaluating elderly persons.

CHAPTER 5

ANALYSIS AND DISCUSSION OF RESULTS

The chapter is devoted to a presentation of the results in relation to each of the hypotheses; additional data are also reported. Each hypothesis is stated separately and followed by the analysis.

Hypothesis 1

HO: Null Hypothesis:
There will be no difference in the responses of preschool children in a Foster Grandparent Day Care Program (Group A) perceptions toward the aging and the elderly and those preschool children in regular day care facilities (Group B).

HI: Alternative Hypothesis:
Preschool children enrolled in a Foster Grandparent Day Care Program (Group A) will evidence a difference in perceptions of the aging and the elderly than preschool children enrolled in regular day care facilities.

The statistic used to test the difference between scores of the two groups was a nonparametric difference test, the Wilcoxen t-test. The value of ω is equivalent to the number of times that a score in one group ranks higher than a score in a second group. In Table 5.1 the value of ω, the rank sum, and the exact two-tailed probability are shown. Analysis indicated no significant difference between Group A and Group B. Thus the null hypothesis for Hypothesis I was not rejected by the findings in this study.

When means of the bipolar adjective scores were analyzed, Group A had somewhat higher mean scores for eight of the ten bipolar adjectives on the semantic differential subtest. This finding indicates a less positive view of elderly persons for Group A even though the difference was not significant. Mean responses of Group A and Group B on the semantic differential about the elderly are shown in Table 5.2.

Conducting a profile analysis using the sign test by plotting the means, differences or similarities in the profile

52

can be observed. If there are consistently greater means for one group than for the other group such that their profiles tend to stand apart, the statistical probability of such a consistent difference can be tested by referring to a Bionominal Probability Table according to Isaac and Michael (1971). Therefore, a profile comparison of mean responses of Group A and Group B is shown in Figure 5.1. The probability that Group A would consistently fall to one side of all of the response means of Group B was at the level of significance (p = .05). These findings indicate that children in the Foster Grandparent Day Care Program (Group A) have less positive views of elderly persons than children in regular day care settings (Group B), although the difference in the means was not significant.

TABLE 5.1
RESULTS OF THE WILCOXEN t-TEST FOR SCORES OF GROUP A AND GROUP B ON THE SEMANTIC DIFFERENTIALS ABOUT ELDERLY PERSONS
N = 44

Bipolar Adjectives	Mean Rank of Group A	Mean Rank of Group B	U	Rank Sum W	Probability (2-tailed)
1. Helpful-Harmful	23.3	21.7	223.5	476.5	.6481
2. Healthy-Sick	22.1	22.9	250.5	503.5	.8382
3. Rich-Poor	21.4	23.6	266.0	519.0	.5599
4. Clean-Dirty	24.9	20.1	190.0	443.0	.2077
5. Friendly-Unfriendly	22.9	22.1	251.5	504.5	.8143
6. Pretty-Ugly	23.9	21.1	212.0	465.0	.4687
7. Wonderful-Terrible	23.2	21.8	226.0	479.0	.6945
8. Right-Wrong	23.0	22.0	231.0	484.0	.7835
9. Happy-Sad	22.6	22.4	240.5	493.5	.9704
10. Good-Bad	23.0	22.0	230.0	483.0	.7532

NOTE: Group A (N=22)   Group B (N=22)

TABLE 5.2
MEAN RESPONSES OF GROUP A AND GROUP B ON THE SEM-
ANTIC DIFFERENTIAL ABOUT ELDERLY PERSONS

	Helpful-Harmful	Healthy-Sick	Rich-Poor	Clean-Dirty	Friendly-Unfriendly	Pretty-Ugly	Wonderful-Terrible	Right-Wrong	Happy-Sad	Good-Bad
Group A	2.32	2.77	2.90	3.14	2.55	3.09	2.86	2.40	3.09	2.45
Group B	2.14	2.86	2.95	2.36	2.40	2.36	2.31	1.77	2.45	2.40

Semantic Differential Scale

Fig. 5.1. Profile Comparison of Mean Responses of
Preschool Children in a Foster Grandparent Program (Group A)
and Preschool Children in Regular Day Care Facilities
(Group B) (p = .05).

Hypothesis 2

HO: Null Hypothesis:
There will be no difference in the variety of perceptions in the responses of preschool children in
a Foster Grandparent Day Care (Group A) toward the
aging and the elderly and those preschool children
in regular day care facilities (Group B).

HI: Alternative Hypothesis:
Preschool children enrolled in a Foster Grandparent
Day Care Program (Group A) will evidence a greater
variety of perceptions toward the aging and the
elderly than preschool children in regular day care
facilities (Group B).

The Wilcoxen t-test statistic was utilized to test the
difference between Groups A and B. On each of the cognitive
components: affective-positive; affective-negative; physi-
cal-positive; physical-negative; behavior-positive; and
behavior-negative, the scores of the two groups appear to be
similar as shown in Table 5.3. Thus, the null hypothesis for
Hypothesis 2 was not rejected at alpha level .05. Group A
and Group B were not significantly different in varieties of
perceptions. Further analysis was done in order to get a
total look at children's perceptions of elderly persons.

TABLE 5.3

RESULTS OF THE WILCOXEN t-TEST FOR SCORES ON GROUP A AND
GROUP B ON THE VARIETIES OF PERCEPTIONS
ABOUT ELDERLY PERSONS

Cognitive Component	Mean Rank of Group A	Mean Rank of Group B	U	W	Proba-bility (2-tailed)
Affective-positive	21.5	23.5	264.5	517.5	.2894
Affective-negative	23.0	22.8	231.0	484.	.6386
Physical-positive	21.5	23.5	264.0	517.	.2998
Physical-negative	23.4	21.6	222.0	475.	.5665
Behavior-positive	24.4	20.6	200.0	453.	.2579
Behavior-negative	21.3	23.8	269.5	522.5	.4920

Group A and Group B scores on the cognitive components of the Word Association Subtest were tabulated and combined. The results are shown in Table 5.4. The findings indicate that 90.9 percent of the children made no affective positive remarks and 88.6 percent made no affective-negative remarks about elderly persons. However, on the physical dimension 31.8 percent of the children made negative evaluations compared to only 9.1 percent of the children who made positive physical comments about the elderly person. The most striking comparison was found in the behavioral dimensions. A total of 38.6 percent of the children had some positive description whereas 59.1 percent of the children made negative evaluations. The range was from one to six different behavioral descriptive evaluations. In the realistic component category, 34.1 percent of the children had no response, whereas over half of the children (52.3%) made at least one evaluation.

The data indicate that more children express negative responses than positive responses about elderly persons in all three components - affective, physical, and behavioral. Children make more negative responses in describing the behavioral component of elderly persons followed by the physical component.

Hypothesis 3

HO: Null Hypothesis:
There will be no difference in the reported amount of direct contact with the aging and the elderly of preschool children in a Foster Grandparent Day Care Program and preschool children in regular day care facilities.

HI: Alternative Hypothesis:
Preschool children in the Foster Grandparent Day Care Program (Group A) will evidence greater amount of direct contact with the aging and the elderly than children in regular day care facilities (Group B).

The statistic used to test the difference between scores of the two groups was a nonparametric difference test, the Wilcoxen t-test. Analysis of the data indicated there was no significant difference between Group A and Group B ($p \geq .05$). Thus, Hypothesis 3 was not supported by the findings in this study. Therefore, the null hypothesis was not

TABLE 5.4

RANGE AND FREQUENCY COUNT OF CHILDREN'S RESPONSES ON THE
VARIETY OF PERCEPTIONS ABOUT ELDERLY PERSONS

Group	0	1	2	3	4	5	6	7	8
	Frequency Count of Responses								

Group	Frequency Count of Responses 0	1	2	3	4	5	6	7	8
Affective Components									
Number of children Positive	40 (90.9%)	3 (6.8%)	1 (2.3%)						
Negative	39 (88.6%)	5 (11.4%)							
Physical Component									
Number of children Positive	39 (88.6%)	4 (9.1%)							
Negative	29 (65.9%)	10 (22.7%)	4 (9.1%)						
Behavioral Component									
Number of children Positive	27 (61.4%)	8 (18.2%)	7 (15.9%)	1 (2.3%)		1 (2.3%)			
Negative	18 (40.9%)	16 (36.4%)	5 (11.4%)	2 (4.5%)	1 (2.3%)	1 (2.3%)			
Realistic Component									
Number of children Neutral	15 (34.1%)	23 (52.3%)	3 (6.8%)	2 (4.5%)	1 (2.3%)				

rejected for Hypothesis 3.

TABLE 5.5
RESULTS OF THE WILCOXEN TEST FOR SCORES OF GROUP A AND GROUP B ON THE AMOUNT OF DIRECT CONTACT WITH ELDERLY PERSONS

Groups	Mean Rank of Group A	Mean Rank of Group B	U	W	Probability (2-tailed)
55-65 years					
Males	22.3	22.7	246.5	499.5	.9140
Females	22.0	23.0	252.0	505.0	.8103
66-75 years					
Males	22.5	22.5	242.0	495.0	1.000
Females	21.8	23.2	257.5	510.5	.7106
76 years and older					
Males	22.8	22.2	234.5	487.5	.8535
Females	22.0	23.0	253.0	506.0	.7894

rejected for Hypothesis 3.

Hypothesis 4

HO: Null Hypothesis:
There will be no difference in the response of children in the Foster Grandparent Day Care Program (Group A) and children in regular day care program (Group B) on feelings about getting old themselves.

HI: Alternative Hypothesis:
Preschool children in Group A will evidence more positive feelings about getting old themselves than Group B.

Scores are tabulated as good, doesn't matter, and bad for Group A and Group B in Table 5.6. A larger percentage of Group A (36.4%) rated themselves as having a good feeling about getting old whereas 27.2 percent of the children in Group B felt good. Half of the children in Group B (50%) rated the feelings they had about getting old as bad whereas 36.4 percent in Group A rated themselves this way. Children in Group A had more positive feelings about getting old themselves than Group B.

TABLE 5.6

DISTRIBUTION OF SCORES FOR GROUP A AND GROUP B ON THE WORD ASSOCIATION SUBTEST ON FEELINGS ABOUT GETTING OLD

| | Feelings | | | |
	Good	Doesn't Matter	Bad	Mean
Group A	8	6	8	2.0
Group B	6	5	11	2.23
N = 44				

Means and percentages were used as the decision rule for this hypothesis. The group with a larger percentage of children with more positive scores and a smaller percentage of children with negative scores indicated a more positive feeling about getting old themselves. The null hypothesis for Hypothesis 4 was rejected.

Hypothesis 5

HO: Null Hypothesis:
There will be no relationship of the responses of children's perceptions of grandparents to children's perceptions of elderly persons.

HI: Alternative Hypothesis:
Children's perceptions of grandparents will show a relationship to children's perceptions of elderly persons.

Group A and Group B scores were tabulated and combined to produce a group score about children's perceptions of elderly persons and grandparents for each of the ten bipolar adjectives of the semantic differential subtest. Children's perceptual response scores of elderly persons and of grandparents were tested using the nonparametric rank-order Kendall's tau correlational technique.

The Kendall's tau statistical indices reflect the direction of the relationship that appears to exist, the tendency toward linear relationship between variables, and the monotonicity of the underlying relation. High positive values suggest that the relation tends to be monotone - increasing, high negative values suggest monotone - decreasing and small absolute or zero values of these indices suggest either that the two variables are not related at all or that the form of the relation is monotone (Hayes, 1973). The Kendall tau findings are shown in Table 5.7.

TABLE 5.7

KENDALL'S TAU C SHOWING CONCORDANCE ON CHILDREN'S PERCEPTIONS OF ELDERLY AND GRANDPARENTS ON THE BIPOLAR ADJECTIVES OF THE SEMANTIC DIFFERENTIAL

Bipolar Adjectives	Coefficient Indices	Significance
Good-Bad	.1072	.104
Happy-Sad	.0336	.374
Right-Wrong	.1304	.138
Wonderful-Terrible	0	.500
Pretty-Ugly	.0785	.210
Friendly-Unfriendly	.1950	.016*
Clean-Dirty	.1550	.061**
Rich-Poor	.0801	.219
Healthy-Sick	-.0555	.295
Helpful-Harmful	.0785	.155

*Significant at the .05 level.
**Tendency towards the significance.

Only on one pair of the bipolar adjectives, friendly-unfriendly, was there a significant tendency of concordance between children's perceptions of elderly persons and children's perceptions of grandparents. Therefore, the null hypothesis, Hypothesis 5, is only partially supported. The bipolar adjectives, clean-dirty, have a tendency toward significance. The interesting negative coefficient value -.0555 for the bipolar adjectives healthy-sick suggests that an increase in the value of X domain is accompanied by a decrease in the value of Y (Monotone-decreasing). The zero value of the bipolar adjectives wonderful-terrible suggests either that the two variables are not related at all or that the form of the relation is nonmonotone (a function that plots as a parabola). Thus, the null hypothesis for Hypothesis 5 was not entirely rejected.

Additional Statistical Tests to Further Evaluate the Data

Since the null hypothesis (Hypothesis 5) was not entirely rejected, a further look at the data was necessary.

Cross Tabulation
Children's perceptual response scores of elderly persons and of grandparents were cross tabulated for each bipolar adjective. The cross tabulations for each are found in Tables 5.8 - 5.17.

Sign Test of the Profile Pattern
The sign test of the profile pattern was also carried out and is shown in Figure 5.2.

The probability that all of the response medians of children's perceptions of grandparents would consistently fall to one side of all of the response means of children's perceptions of elderly persons is P = .001 (a no cross-over pattern). Children's perceptions of grandparents were consistently more positive than children's perceptions of elderly. The difference between children's ratings of grandparents and elderly persons on the positive side of the right-wrong pair of adjectives was very small.

Hypothesis 6

HO: Null Hypothesis:
There will be no difference in children's perceptual responses about elderly persons and parents' responses about the elderly.

HI: Alternative Hypothesis:
Children's perceptual responses about elderly persons will show a difference from parents' responses about the elderly.

The Wilcoxen t-test for two matched samples was used to test the hypothesis that the two populations represented by the respective members of matched pairs, parents and children, are identical. The sign difference between each parent-child dyad observation was found. Then, these differences

TABLE 5.8
CROSS TABULATIONS OF CHILDREN'S RATINGS ON PERCEPTIONS OF
GRANDPARENTS AND ELDERLY PERSONS ON THE BIPOLAR-ADJECTIVES,
GOOD-BAD

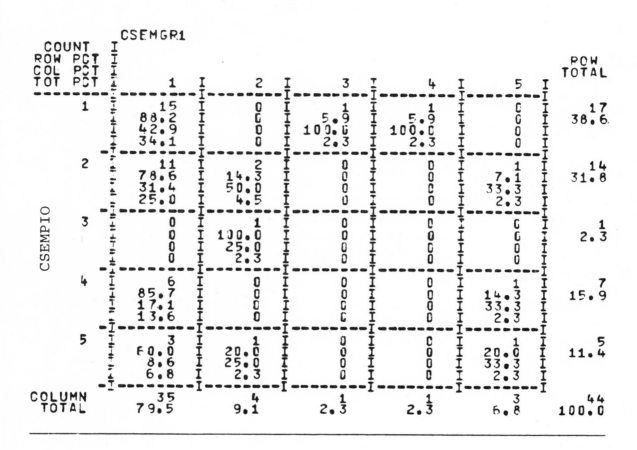

COUNT ROW PCT COL PCT TOT PCT	CSEMGR1 1	2	3	4	5	ROW TOTAL
1	15 88.2 42.9 34.1	0 0 0 0	1 5.9 100.0 2.3	1 5.9 100.0 2.3	0 0 0 0	17 38.6
2	11 78.6 31.4 25.0	2 14.3 50.0 4.5	0 0 0 0	0 0 0 0	1 7.1 33.3 2.3	14 31.8
3	0 0 0 0	1 100.0 25.0 2.3	0 0 0 0	0 0 0 0	0 0 0 0	1 2.3
4	6 85.7 17.1 13.6	0 0 0 0	0 0 0 0	0 0 0 0	1 14.3 33.3 2.3	7 15.9
5	3 60.0 8.6 6.8	1 20.0 25.0 2.3	0 0 0 0	0 0 0 0	1 20.0 33.3 2.3	5 11.4
COLUMN TOTAL	35 79.5	4 9.1	1 2.3	1 2.3	3 6.8	44 100.0

CSEMPIO (row variable, left axis)

NOTE: CSEMGRI = Childrens' Ratings of Grandparents
      CSEMPIO = Childrens' Ratings of Edlerly Persons

TABLE 5.9

CROSS TABULATIONS OF CHILDREN'S RATINGS ON PERCEPTIONS OF
GRANDPARENTS AND ELDERLY PERSONS ON THE BIPOLAR-
ADJECTIVES, HAPPY-SAD

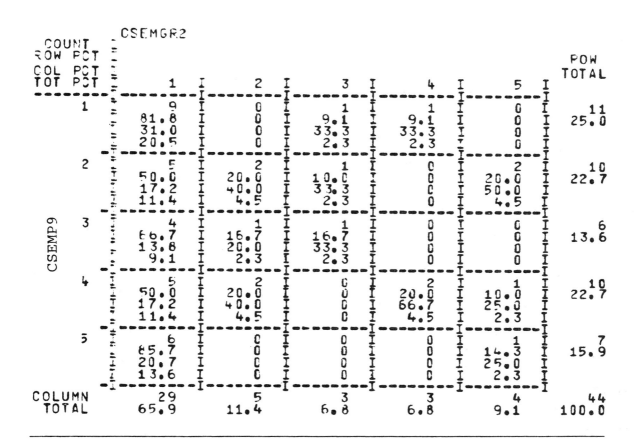

COUNT ROW PCT COL PCT TOT PCT	CSEMGR2 1	2	3	4	5	ROW TOTAL
1	9 81.8 31.0 20.5	0 0 0 0	1 9.1 33.3 2.3	1 9.1 33.3 2.3	0 0 0 0	11 25.0
2	5 50.0 17.2 11.4	2 20.0 40.0 4.5	1 10.0 33.3 2.3	0 0 0 0	2 20.0 50.0 4.5	10 22.7
3	4 66.7 13.8 9.1	1 16.7 20.0 2.3	1 16.7 33.3 2.3	0 0 0 0	0 0 0 0	6 13.6
4	5 50.0 17.2 11.4	2 20.0 40.0 4.5	0 0 0 0	2 20.0 66.7 4.5	1 10.0 25.0 2.3	10 22.7
5	6 85.7 20.7 13.6	0 0 0 0	0 0 0 0	0 0 0 0	1 14.3 25.0 2.3	7 15.9
COLUMN TOTAL	29 65.9	5 11.4	3 6.8	3 6.8	4 9.1	44 100.0

CSEMP9 (rows)

NOTE: CSEMGR2 = Children's Ratings of Grandparents
(columns)
CSEMP9 = Children's Ratings of Elderly Persons
(rows)

TABLE 5.10
CROSS TABULATIONS OF CHILDREN'S RATINGS ON PERCEPTIONS OF GRANDPARENTS AND ELDERLY PERSONS ON THE BIPOLAR-ADJECTIVES, RIGHT-WRONG

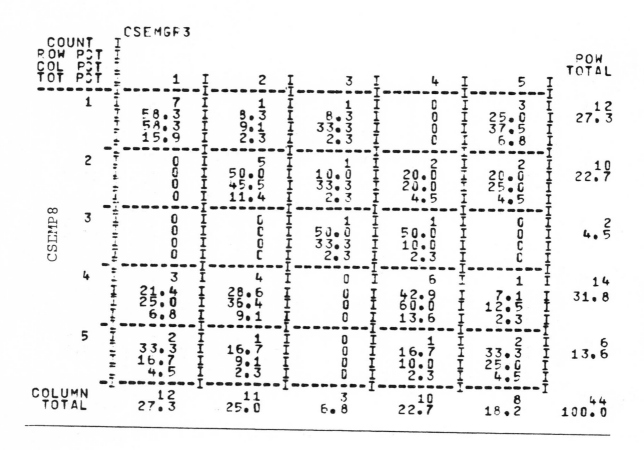

CSEMGR3						
COUNT ROW PCT COL PCT TOT PCT	1	2	3	4	5	ROW TOTAL
1	7 58.3 58.3 15.9	1 8.3 9.1 2.3	1 8.3 33.3 2.3	0 0 0 0	3 25.0 37.5 6.8	12 27.3
2	0 0 0 0	5 50.0 45.5 11.4	1 10.0 33.3 2.3	2 20.0 20.0 4.5	2 20.0 25.0 4.5	10 22.7
3	0 0 0 0	0 0 0 0	1 50.0 33.3 2.3	1 50.0 10.0 2.3	0 0 0 0	2 4.5
4	3 21.4 25.0 6.8	4 28.6 36.4 9.1	0 0 0 0	6 42.9 60.0 13.6	1 7.1 12.5 2.3	14 31.8
5	2 33.3 16.7 4.5	1 16.7 9.1 2.3	0 0 0 0	1 16.7 10.0 2.3	2 33.3 25.0 4.5	6 13.6
COLUMN TOTAL	12 27.3	11 25.0	3 6.8	10 22.7	8 18.2	44 100.0

NOTE: CSEMGR3 = Children's Ratings of Grandparents
                (columns)
        CSEMP8 = Children's Ratings of Elderly Persons
                (rows)

TABLE 5.11
CROSS TABULATIONS OF CHILDREN'S RATINGS ON PERCEPTIONS OF GRANDPARENTS AND ELDERLY PERSONS ON THE BIPOLAR-ADJECTIVES, WONDERFUL-TERRIBLE

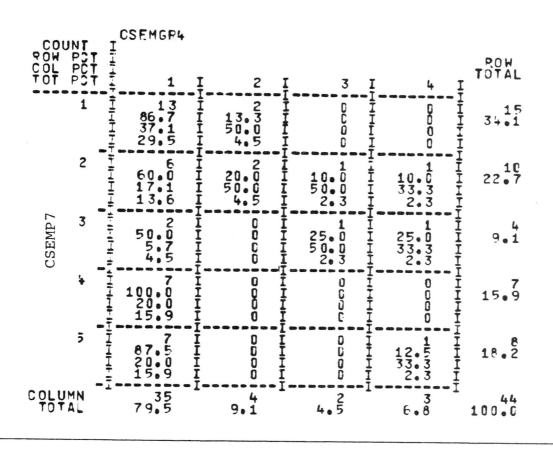

NOTE: CSEMGR4 = Children's Ratings of Grandparents
             (columns)
        CSEMP7 = Children's Ratings of Elderly Persons
             (rows)

65

TABLE 5.12
CROSS TABULATIONS OF CHILDREN'S RATINGS ON PERCEPTIONS OF GRANDPARENTS AND ELDERLY PERSONS ON THE BIPOLAR-ADJECTIVES, PRETTY-UGLY

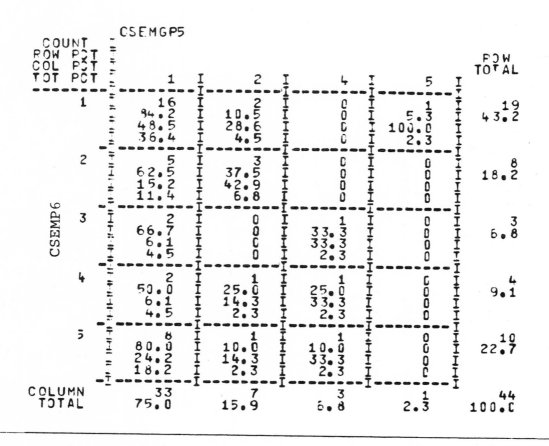

NOTE: CSEMGR5 = Children's Ratings of Grandparents
                  (columns)
        CSEMP6 = Children's Ratings of Elderly Persons
                  (rows)

TABLE 5.13
CROSS TABULATIONS OF CHILDREN'S RATINGS ON PERCEPTIONS OF GRANDPARENTS AND ELDERLY PERSONS ON THE BIPOLAR-ADJECTIVES, FRIENDLY-UNFRIENDLY

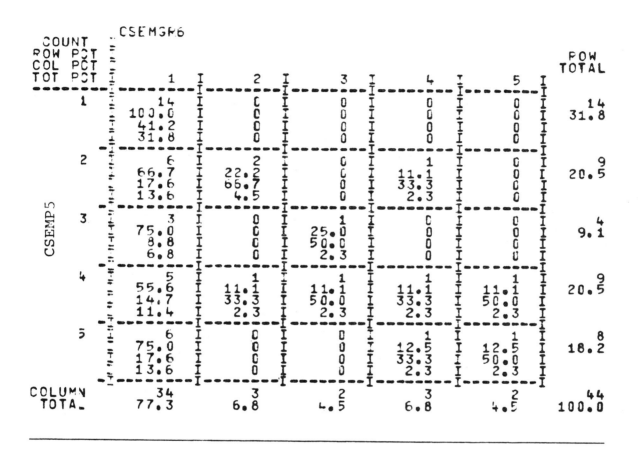

		CSEMGR6					
COUNT ROW PCT COL PCT TOT PCT		1	2	3	4	5	ROW TOTAL
CSEMP5	1	14 100.0 41.2 31.8	0 0 0 0	0 0 0 0	0 0 0 0	0 0 0 0	14 31.8
	2	6 66.7 17.6 13.6	2 22.2 66.7 4.5	0 0 0 0	1 11.1 33.3 2.3	0 0 0 0	9 20.5
	3	3 75.0 8.8 6.8	0 0 0	1 25.0 50.0 2.3	0 0 0	0 0 0	4 9.1
	4	5 55.6 14.7 11.4	1 11.1 33.3 2.3	1 11.1 50.0 2.3	1 11.1 33.3 2.3	1 11.1 50.0 2.3	9 20.5
	5	6 75.0 17.6 13.6	0 0 0	0 0 0	1 12.5 33.3 2.3	1 12.5 50.0 2.3	8 18.2
COLUMN TOTAL		34 77.3	3 6.8	2 4.5	3 6.8	2 4.5	44 100.0

NOTE: CSEMGR6 = Children's Ratings of Grandparents
       (columns)
       CSEMP5 = Children's Ratings of Elderly Persons
       (rows)

TABLE 5.14
CROSS TABULATIONS OF CHILDREN'S RATINGS ON PERCEPTIONS OF GRANDPARENTS AND ELDERLY PERSONS ON THE BIPOLAR-ADJECTIVES, CLEAN-DIRTY

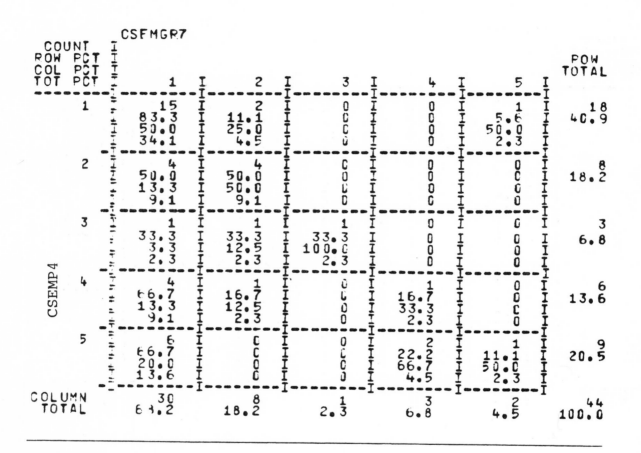

NOTE: CSEMGR7 = Children's Ratings of Grandparents
                 (columns)
       CSEMP4 = Children's Ratings of Elderly Persons
                 (rows)

68

TABLE 5.15
CROSS TABULATIONS OF CHILDREN'S RATINGS ON PERCEPTIONS OF GRANDPARENTS AND ELDERLY PERSONS ON THE BIPOLAR-ADJECTIVES, RICH-POOR

CSEMGR8

COUNT ROW PCT COL PCT TOT PCT	1	2	3	4	5	ROW TOTAL
1	14 70.0 51.9 31.8	5 25.0 45.5 11.4	0 0 0 0	0 0 0 0	1 5.0 33.3 2.3	20 45.5
2	6 50.0 22.2 13.6	5 41.7 45.5 11.4	0 0 0 0	1 8.3 50.0 2.3	0 0 0 0	12 27.3
3	0 0 0 0	0 0 0 0	1 25.0 100.0 2.3	1 25.0 50.0 2.3	2 50.0 66.7 4.5	4 9.1
4	1 50.0 3.7 2.3	1 50.0 9.1 2.3	0 0 0 0	0 0 0 0	0 0 0 0	2 4.5
5	6 100.0 22.2 13.6	0 0 0 0	0 0 0 0	0 0 0 0	0 0 0 0	6 13.6
COLUMN TOTAL	27 61.4	11 25.0	1 2.3	2 4.5	3 6.8	44 100.0

CSEMP3 (rows label)

NOTE: CSEMGR8 = Children's Ratings of Grandparents (columns)

CSEMP3 = Children's Ratings of Elderly Persons (rows)

69

TABLE 5.16

CROSS TABULATIONS OF CHILDREN'S RATINGS ON PERCEPTIONS OF GRANDPARENTS AND ELDERLY PERSONS ON THE BIPOLAR ADJECTIVES, HEALTHY-SICK

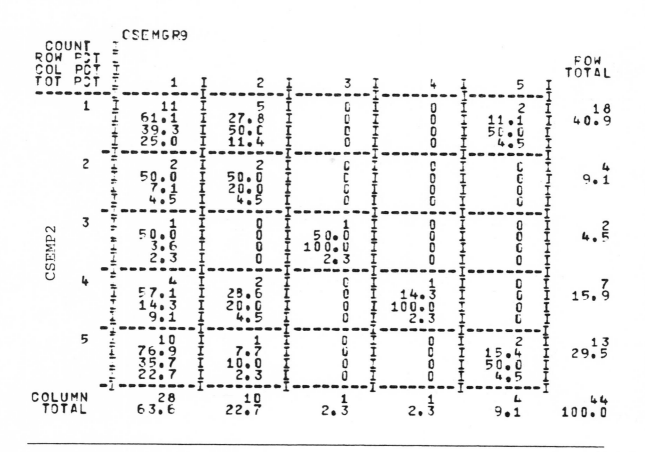

CSEMP2 \ CSEMGR9 COUNT ROW PCT COL PCT TOT PCT	1	2	3	4	5	ROW TOTAL
1	11 61.1 39.3 25.0	5 27.8 50.0 11.4	0 0 0 0	0 0 0 0	2 11.1 50.0 4.5	18 40.9
2	2 50.0 7.1 4.5	2 50.0 20.0 4.5	0 0 0 0	0 0 0 0	0 0 0 0	4 9.1
3	1 50.0 3.6 2.3	0 0 0 0	1 50.0 100.0 2.3	0 0 0 0	0 0 0 0	2 4.5
4	4 57.1 14.3 9.1	2 28.6 20.0 4.5	0 0 0 0	1 14.3 100.0 2.3	0 0 0 0	7 15.9
5	10 76.9 35.7 22.7	1 7.7 10.0 2.3	0 0 0 0	0 0 0 0	2 15.4 50.0 4.5	13 29.5
COLUMN TOTAL	28 63.6	10 22.7	1 2.3	1 2.3	4 9.1	44 100.0

NOTE: CSEMGR9 = Children's Ratings of Grandparents (columns)
CSEMP2 = Children's Ratings of Elderly Persons (rows)

TABLE 5.17
CROSS TABULATIONS OF CHILDREN'S RATINGS ON PERCEPTIONS OF GRANDPARENTS AND ELDERLY PERSONS ON THE BIPOLAR-ADJECTIVES, HELPFUL-HARMFUL

```
                      CSEMGR10

 COUNT    I
 ROW PCT  I                                                          ROW
 COL PCT  I                                                          TOTAL
 TOT PCT  I     1    I     2    I     4    I     5    I
----------I----------I----------I----------I----------I
        1 I    23    I     1    I     0    I     1    I        25
          I  92.0    I   4.0    I   0.0    I   4.0    I      56.8
          I  62.2    I  25.0    I   0.0    I 100.0    I
          I  52.3    I   2.3    I   0.0    I   2.3    I
----------I----------I----------I----------I----------I
        2 I     3    I     3    I     0    I     0    I         6
          I  50.0    I  50.0    I   0.0    I   0.0    I      13.6
          I   8.1    I  75.0    I   0.0    I   0.0    I
          I   6.8    I   6.8    I   0.0    I   0.0    I
----------I----------I----------I----------I----------I
        3 I     1    I     0    I     0    I     0    I         1
          I 100.0    I   0.0    I   0.0    I   0.0    I       2.3
          I   2.7    I   0.0    I   0.0    I   0.0    I
          I   2.3    I   0.0    I   0.0    I   0.0    I
----------I----------I----------I----------I----------I
        4 I     1    I     0    I     1    I     0    I         2
          I  50.0    I   0.0    I  50.0    I   0.0    I       4.5
          I   2.7    I   0.0    I  50.0    I   0.0    I
          I   2.3    I   0.0    I   2.3    I   0.0    I
----------I----------I----------I----------I----------I
        5 I     9    I     0    I     1    I     0    I        10
          I  90.0    I   0.0    I  10.0    I   0.0    I      22.7
          I  24.3    I   0.0    I  50.0    I   0.0    I
          I  20.5    I   0.0    I   2.3    I   0.0    I
----------I----------I----------I----------I----------I
 COLUMN         37         4          2          1            44
 TOTAL        84.1        9.1        4.5        2.3         100.0
```

CSEMP1 (rows)

NOTE   CSEMGR10 = Children's Ratings of Grandparents
(columns)
CSEMP1 = Children's Ratings of Elderly Persons
(rows)

71

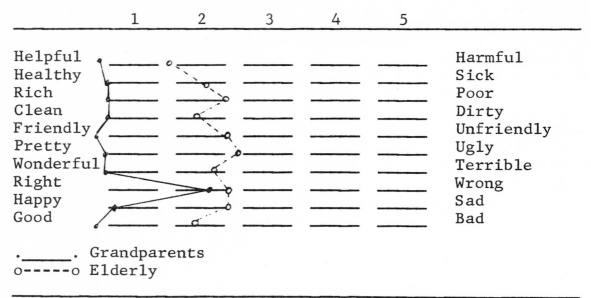

Semantic Differential Scale

._____. Grandparents
o-----o Elderly

Fig. 5.2. The Sign Test of the Profile Pattern
of Median Responses of Children's Perceptions of Elderly
Persons and Grandparents (p = .001).

were rank-ordered in terms of their absolute size, and the
sign of the difference was attached to the rank for their
difference. The final data for the Wilcoxen Matched Pairs,
Signed Rank Test are shown in Table 5.18. This test refers
to the hypothesis that two population distributions of unspe-
cified form are exactly alike. Thus, the null hypothesis of
Hypothesis 6 was not rejected. This implied that the population did not necessarily differ and, therefore, further
analysis was warranted.

TABLE 5.18
WILCOXEN MATCHED PAIRS t-TEST FOR PARENT-CHILD PER-
CEPTIONS OF ELDERLY PERSONS

	-Rank	+Rank	Z	Probability (2-tailed
Total N = 44	18.1	25.9	-1.774	.0761

Additional Information

Sign Test of the Profile Pattern

Group A and Group B scores were tabulated and combined to produce a group score about children's perceptions of elderly persons on each of the bipolar adjectives of the semantic differential subtest. The parents' scores were also tabulated and combined to form a group score about parents' perceptions of elderly persons. The sign test of the profile pattern is shown in Figure 5.3.

The probability that all of the median responses of children's perceptions of elderly persons would consistently fall to one side of all of the median responses of parental perceptions of elderly persons was P = .055. This was an occurrence of eight out of ten bipolar adjectives. Parents' perceptions of elderly on the semantic differential were more positive on eight bipolar adjectives than the children's perceptions. The eight bipolar adjectives were helpful-harmful, healthy-sick, rich-poor, friendly-unfriendly, clean-dirty, pretty-ugly, wonderful-terrible, and happy-sad. Children's perceptions of elderly persons were more positive on the evaluation dimensions of right-wrong and good-bad than parents' perceptions. This supports findings in child development.

Piaget (1932) believed that the child sees rules as external absolutes and feels that parents and other adults are all knowing, perfect, and sacred. Also, according to Kohlberg (1964) this attitude of unilateral respect toward adults, joined with the child's "realism" is believed to lead the child to view rules as sacred and unchangeable. Therefore, the young child views an act as either totally right or totally wrong. If the young child recognizes a conflict in views, the child believes the adult's view is always the right one. This probably accounts for the more positive view of elderly by the children on the right-wrong and good-bad dimensions.

Kendall's tau Correlational Technique

A nonparametric rank-order correlational statistic, Kendall's tau, was used to test the relationship between children's perceptions of elderly persons and parents' perceptions of elderly persons. The findings of the data are reported in Table 5.19. Of the ten bipolar adjectives in the semantic differential, the parents' score and children's score showed a tendency for a relationship about the

Semantic Differential Scale

	1	2	3	4	5	
Helpful						Harmful
Healthy						Sick
Rich						Poor
Friendly						Unfriendly
Clean						Dirty
Pretty						Ugly
Wonderful						Terrible
Right						Wrong
Happy						Sad
Good						Bad

._____. Parents
o------o Children

Figure 5.3.   The Sign Test of the Profile Pattern
of Median Responses of Children's Perceptions of Elderly
Persons and Parental Perceptions of Elderly Persons.

perceptions of elderly persons on four evaluative dimensions
- helpful-harmful, healthy-sick, clean-dirty, and pretty-ugly.
Indications are that parents have an influence on their children's perceptions of elderly persons, however, they are not
completely influential.

TABLE 5.19
KENDALL'S TAU C SHOWING "CONCORDANCE" ON CHILDREN'S PERCEP-
TIONS OF ELDERLY PERSONS AND PARENTS' PERCEPTIONS OF ELDERLY
PERSONS

Bipolar Adjectives	Coefficient Indices	Significance
Helpful-harmful	-.1846	.056*
Healthy-sick	-.1928	.058*
Rich-poor	-.1570	.731
Clean-dirty	-.1897	.073
Friendly-unfriendly	-.0138	.452
Pretty-ugly	.1612	.0970*
Wonderful-terrible	.09091	.2235
Right-wrong	.06749	.2693
Happy-sad	.12397	.1577
Good-bad	.09452	.2240

*Tendency for significance of agreement

74

Cross Tabulations

Children's perceptual response scores of elderly persons and parents' perceptual response scores of elderly persons were cross tabulated for each of the bipolar adjective of the semantic differential subtest. The cross tabulations are found in Tables 5.20 - 5.29.

The results of Hypothesis 7 and 8 will be reported together.

Hypothesis 7

HO: Null Hypothesis:
There will be no difference in the responses of children who spend more time with grandparents than those who spend less time with grandparents.

HI: Alternative Hypothesis:
Children who spend more time with grandparents have a more positive perception of grandparents than those who spend less time with grandparents.

Hypothesis 8

HO: Null Hypothesis:
There will be no difference in the responses of children who spend more time with grandparents on the perception of elderly persons than those children who spend less time with grandparents.

HI: Alternative Hypothesis:
Children who spend more time with grandparents have a more positive perception of elderly persons than those who spend less time with grandparents.

The response mean on the semantic differential was compared for the group with most contact with grandparents and the group with no contact with grandparents on their perceptions of elderly persons and grandparents.

The data are shown in Table 5.30. The lower the mean score the more positive are their perceptions.

Thus, the null hypothesis of Hypothesis 7 was rejected. The null hypothesis of Hypothesis 8 was not rejected. Findings indicate that children who have most contact with grandparents have more negative views of elderly persons and

TABLE 5.20
CROSS TABULATIONS OF CHILDREN'S RATINGS AND PARENTS' RATINGS ON PERCEPTIONS OF ELDERLY PERSONS ON THE BIPOLAR-ADJECTIVES, HELPFUL-HARMFUL

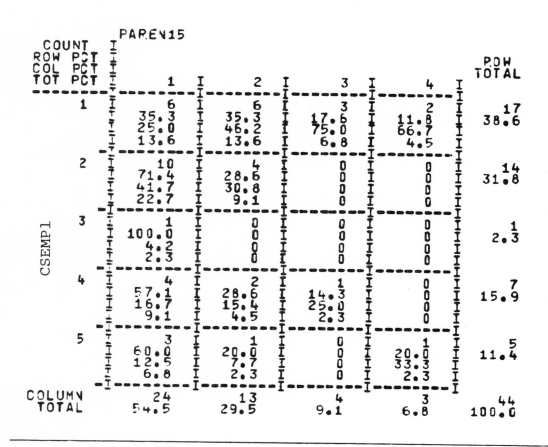

NOTE: PAREN15 = Parents' Rating (columns)
CSEMP1 = Children's Ratings (rows)

76

TABLE 5.21
CROSS TABULATIONS OF CHILDREN'S RATINGS AND PARENTS' RATINGS ON PERCEPTIONS OF ELDERLY PERSONS ON THE BIPOLAR-ADJECTIVES, HEALTHY-SICK

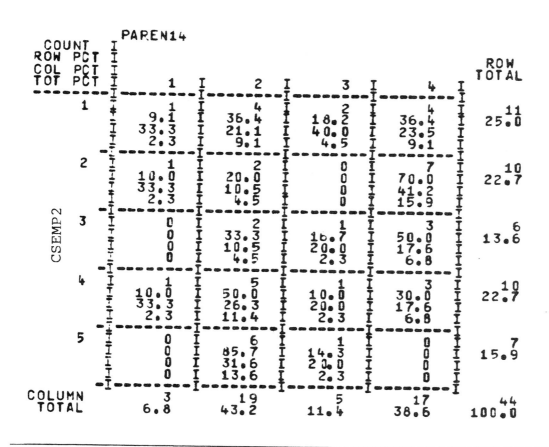

COUNT ROW PCT COL PCT TOT PCT	1	2	3	4	ROW TOTAL
1	1 9.1 33.3 2.3	4 36.4 21.1 9.1	2 18.2 40.0 4.5	4 36.4 23.5 9.1	11 25.0
2	1 10.0 33.3 2.3	2 20.0 10.5 4.5	0 0 0 0	7 70.0 41.2 15.9	10 22.7
3	0 0 0 0	2 33.3 10.5 4.5	1 16.7 20.0 2.3	3 50.0 17.6 6.8	6 13.6
4	1 10.0 33.3 2.3	5 50.0 26.3 11.4	1 10.0 20.0 2.3	3 30.0 17.6 6.8	10 22.7
5	0 0 0 0	6 85.7 31.6 13.6	1 14.3 20.0 2.3	0 0 0 0	7 15.9
COLUMN TOTAL	3 6.8	19 43.2	5 11.4	17 38.6	44 100.0

PAREN14

CSEMP2

NOTE: PAREN14 = Parents' Ratings (columns)
CSEMP2 = Children's Ratings (rows)

TABLE 5.22
CROSS TABULATIONS OF CHILDREN'S RATINGS AND PARENTS' RATINGS
ON PERCEPTIONS OF ELDERLY PERSONS ON THE BIPOLAR-ADJECTIVES,
RICH-POOR

```
                 PAREN12
    COUNT    I
    ROW PCT  I                                                    ROW
    COL PCT  I                                                   TOTAL
    TOT PCT  I      2   I      3   I      4   I      5   I
             I----------I----------I----------I----------I
        1    I      2   I      3   I      5   I      2   I        12
             I   16.7   I   25.0   I   41.7   I   16.7   I   27.3
             I   28.6   I   23.1   I   22.7   I  100.0   I
             I    4.5   I    6.8   I   11.4   I    4.5   I
             I----------I----------I----------I----------I
        2    I      1   I      3   I      6   I      0   I        10
             I   10.0   I   30.0   I   60.0   I      0   I   22.7
             I   14.3   I   23.1   I   27.3   I      0   I
             I    2.3   I    6.8   I   13.6   I      0   I
CSEMP3       I----------I----------I----------I----------I
        3    I      0   I      1   I      1   I      0   I         2
             I      0   I   50.0   I   50.0   I      0   I    4.5
             I      0   I    7.7   I    4.5   I      0   I
             I      0   I    2.3   I    2.3   I      0   I
             I----------I----------I----------I----------I
        4    I      1   I      5   I      8   I      0   I        14
             I    7.1   I   35.7   I   57.1   I      0   I   31.8
             I   14.3   I   38.5   I   36.4   I      0   I
             I    2.3   I   11.4   I   18.2   I      0   I
             I----------I----------I----------I----------I
        5    I      3   I      1   I      2   I      0   I         6
             I   50.0   I   16.7   I   33.3   I      0   I   13.6
             I   42.9   I    7.7   I    9.1   I      0   I
             I    6.8   I    2.3   I    4.5   I      0   I
             I----------I----------I----------I----------I
    COLUMN         7         13         22          2            44
    TOTAL        15.9       29.5       50.0        4.5        100.0
```

NOTE: PAREN12 = Parents' Ratings (columns)
         CSEMP3 = Children's Ratings (rows)

TABLE 5.23
CROSS TABULATIONS OF CHILDREN'S RATINGS AND PARENTS' RATINGS ON PERCEPTIONS OF ELDERLY PERSONS ON THE BIPOLAR-ADJECTIVES, FRIENDLY-UNFRIENDLY

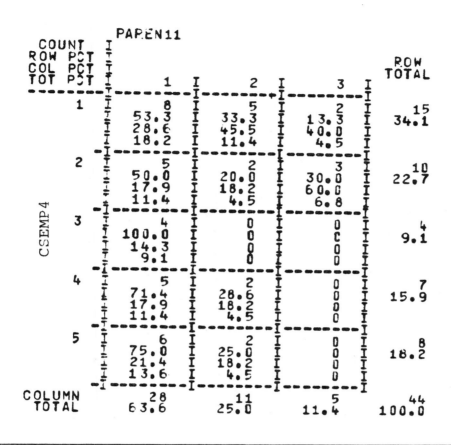

COUNT ROW PCT COL PCT TOT PCT	PAREN11 1	2	3	ROW TOTAL
1	8 53.3 28.6 18.2	5 33.3 45.5 11.4	2 13.3 40.0 4.5	15 34.1
2	5 50.0 17.9 11.4	2 20.0 18.2 4.5	3 30.0 60.0 6.8	10 22.7
3	4 100.0 14.3 9.1	0 0 0 0	0 0 0 0	4 9.1
4	5 71.4 17.9 11.4	2 28.6 18.2 4.5	0 0 0 0	7 15.9
5	6 75.0 21.4 13.6	2 25.0 18.2 4.5	0 0 0 0	8 18.2
COLUMN TOTAL	28 63.6	11 25.0	5 11.4	44 100.0

CSEMP4

NOTE: PAREN11 = Parents' Ratings (columns)
       CSEMP4 = Children's Ratings (rows)

TABLE 5.24

CROSS TABULATIONS OF CHILDREN'S RATINGS AND PARENTS' RATINGS ON PERCEPTIONS OF ELDERLY PERSONS ON THE BIPOLAR-ADJECTIVES, CLEAN-DIRTY

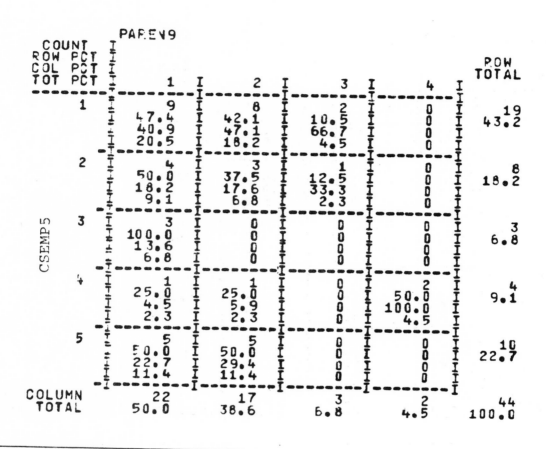

COUNT / ROW PCT / COL PCT / TOT PCT	PAREN9 1	2	3	4	ROW TOTAL
CSEMP5 1	9 47.4 40.9 20.5	8 42.1 47.1 18.2	2 10.5 66.7 4.5	0 0 0 0	19 43.2
2	4 50.0 18.2 9.1	3 37.5 17.6 6.8	1 12.5 33.3 2.3	0 0 0 0	8 18.2
3	3 100.0 13.6 6.8	0 0 0 0	0 0 0 0	0 0 0 0	3 6.8
4	1 25.0 4.5 2.3	1 25.0 5.9 2.3	0 0 0 0	2 50.0 100.0 4.5	4 9.1
5	5 50.0 22.7 11.4	5 50.0 29.4 11.4	0 0 0 0	0 0 0 0	10 22.7
COLUMN TOTAL	22 50.0	17 38.6	3 6.8	2 4.5	44 100.0

NOTE PAREN9 = Parents' Ratings (columns)
CSEMP5 = Children's Ratings (rows)

TABLE 5.25

CROSS TABULATIONS OF CHILDREN'S RATINGS AND PARENTS' RATINGS ON PERCEPTIONS OF ELDERLY PERSONS ON THE BIPOLAR-ADJECTIVES, PRETTY-UGLY

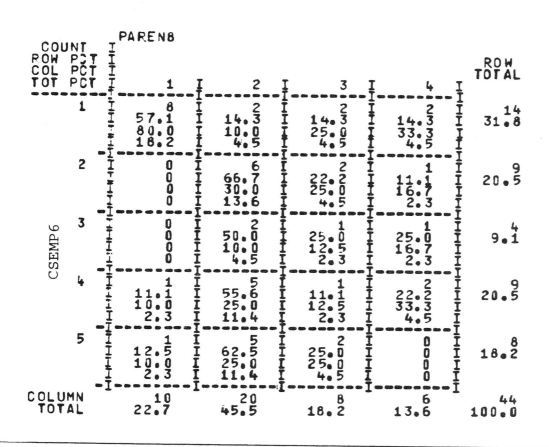

CSEMP6 / PAREN8 (COUNT / ROW PCT / COL PCT / TOT PCT)	1	2	3	4	ROW TOTAL
1	8 57.1 80.0 18.2	2 14.3 10.0 4.5	2 14.3 25.0 4.5	2 14.3 33.3 4.5	14 31.8
2	0 0 0 0	6 66.7 30.0 13.6	2 22.2 25.0 4.5	1 11.1 16.7 2.3	9 20.5
3	0 0 0 0	2 50.0 10.0 4.5	1 25.0 12.5 2.3	1 25.0 16.7 2.3	4 9.1
4	1 11.1 10.0 2.3	5 55.6 25.0 11.4	1 11.1 12.5 2.3	2 22.2 33.3 4.5	9 20.5
5	1 12.5 10.0 2.3	5 62.5 25.0 11.4	2 25.0 25.0 4.5	0 0 0 0	8 18.2
COLUMN TOTAL	10 22.7	20 45.5	8 18.2	6 13.6	44 100.0

NOTE: PAREN8 = Parents' Ratings (columns)
CSEMP6 = Children's Ratings (rows)

TABLE 5.26
CROSS TABULATIONS OF CHILDREN'S RATINGS AND PARENTS' RATINGS ON PERCEPTIONS OF ELDERLY PERSONS ON THE BIPOLAR-ADJECTIVES, WONDERFUL-TERRIBLE

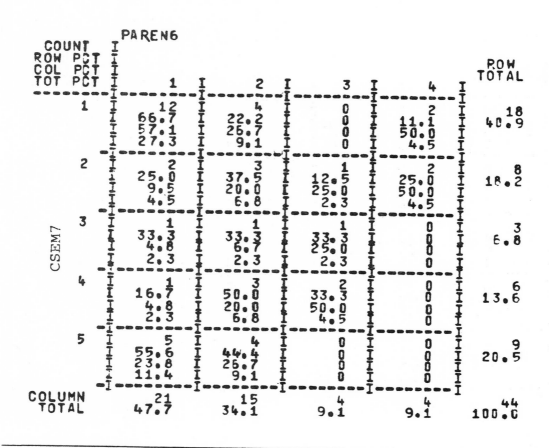

COUNT ROW PCT COL PCT TOT PCT	PAREN6 1	2	3	4	ROW TOTAL
1	12 66.7 57.1 27.3	4 22.2 26.7 9.1	0 0 0 0	2 11.1 50.0 4.5	18 40.9
2	2 25.0 9.5 4.5	3 37.5 20.0 6.8	1 12.5 25.0 2.3	2 25.0 50.0 4.5	8 18.2
3	1 33.3 4.8 2.3	1 33.3 6.7 2.3	1 33.3 25.0 2.3	0 0 0	3 6.8
4	1 16.7 4.8 2.3	3 50.0 20.0 6.8	2 33.3 50.0 4.5	0 0 0	6 13.6
5	5 55.6 23.8 11.4	4 44.4 26.7 9.1	0 0 0	0 0 0	9 20.5
COLUMN TOTAL	21 47.7	15 34.1	4 9.1	4 9.1	44 100.0

CSEM7 (rows)

NOTE: PAREN6 = Parents' Ratings (columns)
CSEM7 = Children's Ratings (rows)

82

TABLE 5.27
CROSS TABULATIONS OF CHILDREN'S RATINGS AND PARENTS' RATINGS ON PERCEPTIONS OF ELDERLY PERSONS ON THE BIPOLAR-ADJECTIVES, RIGHT-WRONG

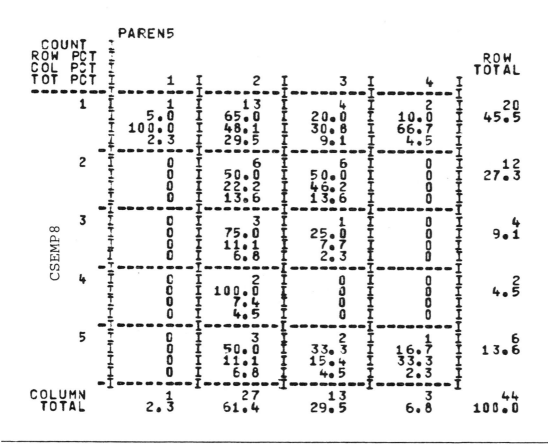

PAREN5

COUNT ROW PCT COL PCT TOT PCT	1	2	3	4	ROW TOTAL
1	1 5.0 100.0 2.3	13 65.0 48.1 29.5	4 20.0 30.8 9.1	2 10.0 66.7 4.5	20 45.5
2	0 0 0 0	6 50.0 22.2 13.6	6 50.0 46.2 13.6	0 0 0 0	12 27.3
3	0 0 0 0	3 75.0 11.1 6.8	1 25.0 7.7 2.3	0 0 0 0	4 9.1
4	0 0 0 0	2 100.0 7.4 4.5	0 0 0	0 0 0	2 4.5
5	0 0 0 0	3 50.0 11.1 6.8	2 33.3 15.4 4.5	1 16.7 33.3 2.3	6 13.6
COLUMN TOTAL	1 2.3	27 61.4	13 29.5	3 6.8	44 100.0

CSEMP8 *(row variable label)*

NOTE PAREN5 = Parents' Ratings (columns)
CSEMP8 = Children's Ratings (rows)

83

TABLE 5.28
CROSS TABULATIONS OF CHILDREN'S RATINGS AND PARENTS' RATINGS ON PERCEPTIONS OF ELDERLY PERSONS ON THE BIPOLAR-ADJECTIVES, HAPPY-SAD

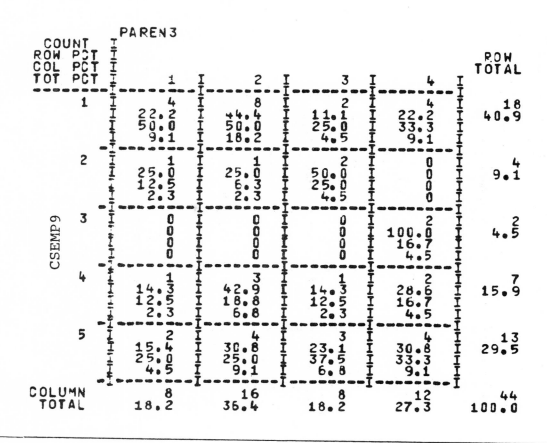

	PAREN3				
COUNT ROW PCT COL PCT TOT PCT	1	2	3	4	ROW TOTAL
1	4 22.2 50.0 9.1	8 44.4 50.0 18.2	2 11.1 25.0 4.5	4 22.2 33.3 9.1	18 40.9
2	1 25.0 12.5 2.3	1 25.0 6.3 2.3	2 50.0 25.0 4.5	0 0 0 0	4 9.1
3	0 0 0 0	0 0 0 0	0 0 0 0	2 100.0 16.7 4.5	2 4.5
4	1 14.3 12.5 2.3	3 42.9 18.8 6.8	1 14.3 12.5 2.3	2 28.6 16.7 4.5	7 15.9
5	2 15.4 25.0 4.5	4 30.8 25.0 9.1	3 23.1 37.5 6.8	4 30.8 33.3 9.1	13 29.5
COLUMN TOTAL	8 18.2	16 36.4	8 18.2	12 27.3	44 100.0

CSEMP9 (rows)

NOTE: PAREN3 = Parents' Ratings (columns)
        CSEMP9 = Children's Ratings (rows)

TABLE 5.29
CROSS TABULATIONS OF CHILDREN'S RATINGS AND PARENTS' RATINGS ON PERCEPTIONS OF ELDERLY PERSONS ON THE BIPOLAR-ADJECTIVES, GOOD-BAD

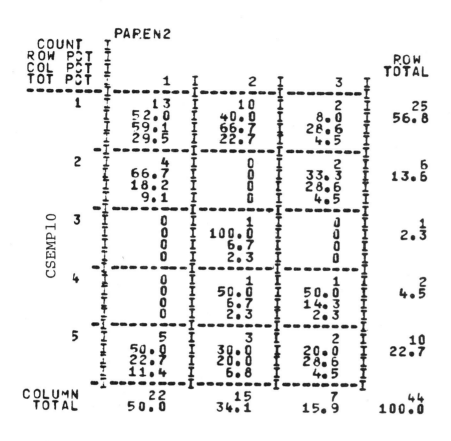

NOTE: PAREN2 = Parents' Ratings (columns)
        CSEMP10 = Children's Ratings (rows)

TABLE 5.30

THE MEAN PERCEPTUAL SCORES OF CHILDREN WHO HAVE MOST CONTACT
AND LESS CONTACT

Group	Elderly Persons Mean Score	Grandparents Mean Score
Most Contact	3.65	1.05
Less Contact	1.3	1.26

a more positive view of grandparents than children who have less contact with grandparents. The mean scores for the children with least contact with grandparents show that their perceptions of the elderly are very similar to their mean score of their perceptions of grandparents.

An interesting phenomenon was the finding that all the children with most contact with grandparents rated both the elderly person as well as grandparents Very Sad on the bi-polar adjective Happy-Sad. Whereas all the children with least contact with grandparents rated the grandparent Very happy and only one child rated the elderly person as very sad. All others also rated the elderly person as Very Happy on the bipolar adjective Happy-Sad. The implications derived from these data need further study.

Additional Information

Further analysis of the data derived from the CATE was necessary to get a more complete picture of children who have most contact with grandparents and of those who have least contact with grandparents about their perceptions of the elderly.

To provide descriptive answers for the hypotheses, a description and discussion of the various data on the CATE instrument are reported for each of the subjects. The children's mean response scores on the Word Association Subtest, Semantic Differential Subtest, and Concrete Representation Subtest were analyzed to assess the differences in perceptual responses of children who had most contact with grandparents as opposed to children who had no contact with grandparents. There were two children, one boy, six years old, and one girl, four years old, who saw all their living grandparents at least once each day. There were three six-year-old boys who never saw any of their living grandparents and, therefore, had the least contact with grandparents.

Word Association Subtest Answers

How the Children Answered the Statements: "Tell me about old people" and "How would you feel when you are old?" Children with Most Contact

Subject 1 - Girl: "They squeeze me, when they hug me. They are not new, their faces are real old. They are bad and turn into old people and they are wrong. They hit me. My grandma hurts me and puts me to bed. She babysits me and never lets me watch TV."
"I don't want to get old. I will feel bad."

Subject 2 - Boy: "They have heart attacks and die. They walk slow. Their skin is bumpy. They have whitish, greyish hair." "I will feel sad."

Children with Least Contact

Subject 1 - Boy: "Well old people are sometimes poor, and have no food and have to hunt for them. Sometimes old people are alone. If they are on welfare, they have no money. They have grey hair and beards. Sometimes they sleep on cots, they have no beds to sleep on and sometimes they sleep on the floors. Some old people are nice and some are mean."
"I will feel bad, cuz you don't have food."

Subject 2 - Boy: "Because there's old, old hair."
"I will feel bad."

Subject 3 - Boy: "Sometimes they need crutches. They go to church. Sometimes they shake. Sometimes they have heart attacks. Some are little, some are big. They have old people all around the world. They have grey hair."
"I will feel sad, I like to be young. I don't want to die."

Findings on the Word Association Subtest

Children with most contact did not differ in mean responses from children with least contact on the affective, physical, and behavioral components. However, the difference occurred in the realistic component. The group with the least contact had approximately four times more neutral descriptive evaluations. This could be accounted for by the differences in ages of the children and supports previous findings in the review of the literature that older children are less global in their perceptions. There were no differences in the total responses for each group.

To the question, "How would you feel when you are old?", all the children answered "bad" or "sad." There was no difference in their responses to that question.

Findings on the Subtest -
Concrete Representations
Answers to questions: "What things would you help this person do?" "What things could this person help you do?"

Children with Most Contact

Subject 1 - Girl: She points to a lady. "She will take me to the store. She will talk to me. She will put me to bed." "She can come to my house and spend the night. She can take me swimming. She can buy me a new bathing suit."

She points to a man: "I can help him when he has hard stuff to do. I can help him make a dog house with a dog inside.
"He can take me swimming and go in the water with me. Pick me up and throw me in. He can watch me when I go to deep water."

Subject 2 - Boy: He points to a lady: "Rake her leaves, mow her lawn, pick flowers for her, get coffee and stuff for her, buy groceries for her."

He points to a man:
"He can give me some money, take me to a place where you can find sand dollars. Just love me!!"

Children with Least Contact

Subject 1 - Boy: points to a man: "I go get the police to help him or else take him home with me or else tell Mom where he could live. I could go get a doctor for

him. He doesn't like to live where it's poor and he should."
"He can be nice to me. He can help me write numbers. He can take me to the beach to find shells. He can teach me how to make sand castles. He can teach me how to make dishes with clay."

The subject was asked what he could do with the elderly females (examiner points to females). The subject answered, "I don't know."

Subject 2 - Boy: He points to a man: "I would play with him football."

He points to a lady.

"I fix her some food."
"She can fix me food."

Subject 3 - Boy: He points to man: "Get him something he wants."

Points to lady:

"She can be with me. Buy me something like a toy. Build me a playhouse."

Discussion of Findings

Children who have most contact with grandparents mention more things they can do with and for elderly persons of both sexes than children who have the least contact. This supports Piaget's Cognitive Theory. As the children acquired more experiences with the elderly, the global interpretations of elderly persons were differentiated, specified, and integrated into their understanding of the elderly person. Therefore, the child with the most contact evaluated and described the elderly person in more detail than the child who had the least contact.

Hypotheses	Decision Rule The Null Hypothesis Was:

H1: There will be no difference in the response of preschool children in a Foster Grandparent Day Care Program (Group A) perceptions toward the aging and the elderly and the preschool children in regular day care facilities (Group B).   Not Rejected

H2: There will be no difference in the variety of perceptions in the responses of preschool children in a Foster Grandparent Day Care (Group A) toward the aging and the elderly and the preschool children in regular day care facilities (Group B).   Not Rejected

H3: There will be no difference in the reported amount of direct contact with the aging and the elderly of preschool children in a Foster Grandparent Day Care Program and preschool children in regular day care facilities.   Not Rejected

H4: There will be no difference in the response of children in the Foster Grandparent Day Care Program and children in regular day care programs on feelings about getting old themselves.   Rejected

H5: There will be no relationship in the responses of children's perceptions of grandparents and children's perceptions of elderly persons.   Rejected

H6: There will be no difference in children's perceptual responses about elderly persons and parents' responses about the elderly.   Not Rejected

Hypotheses	Decision Rule
	The Null Hypothesis Was:

H7: There will be no difference in the responses of children who spend more time with grandparents than those children who spend least time with grandparents.

Not Rejected

H8: There will be no difference in the responses of parents on their perception of elderly persons than those children who spend less time with grandparents.

Rejected

Fig. 5.4. Summary of Hypotheses Tested and the Decision Rule

CHAPTER 6

SUMMARY, CONCLUSIONS, AND IMPLICATIONS

Children enrolled in a Foster Grandparent Day Care Program and children in regular day care facilities did not differ in their perceptions concerning the elderly person. Neither did the groups differ in their variety of perceptions or the amount of contact with elderly persons. However, the children did differ in their feelings about getting old. More children in the regular day care facilities expressed their feelings as "bad" when they viewed the prospects of getting old themselves.

Children's perceptions of grandparents and perceptions of elderly persons showed no relationship on the semantic differential except for one dimension. The scores on the bipolar adjectives friendly-unfriendly showed that children's perceptions of grandparents were in agreement with children's perceptions of elderly persons.

Children's perceptions about elderly persons were not different from parental perceptions. There were tendencies for agreement in relationships in four out of the ten bipolar items on the Kendall tau. The results from this section indicated that parents did influence children's perceptual responses about elderly persons.

Although children have little knowledge of older people in our society, children who had the most contact with elderly persons were able to describe and discuss more things they could do with and for elderly persons than children who had least contact. The more negative evaluations of older persons by those children having more contact with elderly persons may be a matter of cognitive development from a global state to one of greater differentiation and specification (Scarlet, Press, and Crockett, 1971). The children were using surface cues, basically physical and behavioral, to classify and categorize elderly persons. In a previous study by Jantz, Seefeldt, Galper, and Serock (1976), these physical and behavioral cues were oftentimes scored as negative rather than positive by coders because the particular society or researcher had classified these characteristics as negatives. White hair, having wrinkles, walking slow, and sometimes shaking are not necessarily negative descriptions; they only become so when society looks at these traits as negative. The child in fact was seeing cues from which he formed his opinions for classification and clarification. Therefore, this investigator cannot conclude by reporting that children's perceptions of elderly persons were negative. There was a mixture of positive, realistic as well as negative perceptions of the elderly.

The sample consisted of forty-four parent-child dyads from three day care facilities in the Lansing, Michigan district. The children from the center with a Foster Grandparent Program formed Group A and children from two regular day care facilities with no elderly aides present during the day formed the contrast Group B.

The design of this study was based on the static-group comparison. To minimize some of the differences between Group A and Group B, some controls in the selection of the center were implemented such as choosing centers that had a sliding scale for rates and choosing centers that were located within the inner city limits.

Data from the children were obtained by the use of a modified version of the CATE, Children's Attitudes Toward the Elderly by Jantz, Seefeldt, Galper, and Serock (1976). A parent questionnaire designed by the investigator was used to obtain data on the demographic profile of the families and grandparents, attitudes of parents toward elderly persons, and general information on human and nonhuman learning resources in the child's environment. Mothers were the primary respondents (93.2%) to the parent questionnaire.

The statistical procedures used to test the differences in the scores were the Wilcoxen t-test, Kendall tau, Wilcoxen matched t-test, sign profile pattern test, cross tabulations, and means. The alpha level of significance was set at .05 as a basis for the decision to reject the null hypothesis which was analyzed by using inferential statistics. Descriptive data as well as means were also used to further evaluate the data.

Descriptive Conclusions

The descriptive conclusions, based upon the findings from the administration of the CATE, will be discussed under the general questions asked.

What Do Children Know About Elderly Persons?

When children were asked what they knew about old people, children responded with descriptions such as,

They get big as the sky; they have a stick to
walk with; sometimes they have lots of wrinkles;
they wear more clothes to keep warm; sometimes
they don't have a car because they can't drive;
their veins show; they have white hair; they
don't look new.

One five-year-old said:

Grandma has grey hair but wears a wig so we can't
tell she has grey hair. My other grandma died.
I start dreaming about old people when I see them,
and their voice sounds old.

Another four-year-old girl said:

They sigh and goes to bed early.

One five-year-old boy said:

Some could die. They put mail in the mail box.
They get sick and they take medicine. They break
a leg and go to the hospital. They wash hands
before dinner and use soap.

It would be worthwhile to have witnessed all the happenings
this child encountered with elderly persons. This child may
be revealing all the events he is trying to sort out and
classify regarding his perceptions of old people.
    Children indicate by their answers that their knowledge
of elderly persons is complex and often based on behavioral
and physical cues.

How Do Children Feel About Elderly Persons?

    Children have a positive feeling for their grandparents
and a less positive feeling for elderly persons in general.
Children who had spend most time with grandparents viewed
other elderly persons with less positive perceptions than
other children. Children who spent the least amount of time
with grandparents viewed grandparents and elderly persons
similarly. This supports the theory that children's perceptions are global in nature, and with more experiences and
contacts these global perceptions become differentiated,
specified, and integrated (Langer, 1970).

Before being shown concrete representations of elderly persons, 43.2 percent of the children perceived growing old as negative. A greater number of children, 56.8 percent, perceived growing old as positive or as neither positive nor negative. However, after looking at the picture of elderly persons on the cover of a magazine, 54.5 percent of the children perceived growing old as negative and 45.4 percent said positive or it didn't matter. There was just a slight change in the scores after the representations were shown.

What Contacts Do Children Have with Elderly Persons?

It seems that children have very limited contact with elderly persons. More children saw elderly females each day than elderly males. Only a few children (three) saw elderly females seventy-six years and over each day. No children saw elderly males seventy-six years and over. Most children (86.4%) saw their grandparent(s) at least once each week.

Parents have difficulty assessing elderly-child interaction. Data indicate that 11.4 percent of the parent respondents were not even aware of the elderly volunteers at the day care centers in which their child was enrolled. It appears parents have very limited knowledge of what happens at the day care centers. Parents also reported very low contact frequencies between their child and other elderly persons from the child's social environment. Whether this finding indicates low elderly-child contact or that parents are not aware of the child's experiences is a question that needs to be answered in order to help explain the child's perceptions.

Children indicate a variety of activities they could do to help elderly persons. Children responded with statements such as:

> Help her put on her necklace; do the dishes; play
> with her; help him be careful with the plates;
> make him happy; paint his house for him; I put
> toys away when I'm done playing so she won't have
> to put them away; get her some food; help her with
> the groceries; get her a frigerator, a stove and
> some chairs; go buy flowers for her; if he taught
> me all those things and couldn't do it anymore,
> I would do it for him; help him saw, chop down
> trees and hammer wood; could fix her up, if her

heart stops; (and quite a few children replied)
I don't know.

Children also indicated a variety of activities that elderly
persons could help the children do such as:

She can help me make things; she can fix lunch;
can fix the car then I let her fix the patio;
then if she won't do it, I kick her; he can
tickle me; teach me how to make money; teach
me how to read books; give me some money to buy
sunglasses.

One three-year-old boy said:

He can teach me to play football and basketball
like Erwin Johnson.

Another five-year-old boy answered:

She can kiss me goodnight.

The descriptive data show that children's perceptions of
elderly persons are egocentric. The perceptions are not just
a matter of stereotypes that the child has been influenced by,
but also involve some previous understanding of the elderly
person's role.

Implications For Future Research

As a result of this study, the investigator recommends
further research on three types: (1) research that is similar to this study but aimed at increasing the knowledge base
about children's perceptions of persons; (2) research which
is generally similar but which eliminates some of the limitations of this study; and (3) research that is very similar
but cross cultural in design.

Research Related Closely to This Study

1. The study should be repeated using a planned curriculum intervention of elderly persons into a day care
setting with a quasi-experimental pretest post-test design.
2. The study should be repeated using a larger sample
of preschool children controlling for race, sex, and

socioeconomic status.

   3.   The study should be repeated contrasting an urban
and rural sample of children.

   4.   The study should be set up so that an interview and
observation procedures are used rather than a questionnaire
instrumentation. The goal would be to see if parents are
better able to recall certain indirect experiences of their
children using the probing technique which may be utilized
when using an interview. Observations may reveal other kinds
of data.

   5.   The study should be repeated recording on tape all
the children's responses to the questions found in the CATA.

   6.   If research on children's perceptions about elderly
persons is to continue, the instruments will need to be
refined. More reliability and validity measures should be
carried out especially in coding the open-ended questions on
both instruments.

Research Related to Increasing the
Knowledge Base

   1.   Using the same sample, a follow-up study about
children's perceptions of elderly in about two to three years
from now is recommended. Studies (Klausemier and Ripple, 1971)
indicate that a child's attitudes develop early in life and
remain as stable enduring parts of the child. Therefore, a
longitudinal study can shed some light as to the stability
of children's perceptions about elderly persons and whether
these perceptions are incorporated into attitudes found in
later life.

   2.   Studies should be devised to determine the impor-
tance of sex, age, and socioeconomic status on children's
perceptions of elderly persons or persons in general.

   3.   Studies should be devised to determine the impor-
tance of visual and behavioral experiences on children's
perceptions of elderly persons.

   4.   Studies should be devised to determine what are the
most important variables that affect blind children's perceptions of elderly persons.

   5.   It is often assumed that preschool children are not
capable of the "highest" type of "rational-altruistic thinking"
(Goodman, 1970). The universal assumption of age/stage
linkages in developmental phases succeeding one another in
order is widely accepted. However, this never explains the
cross cultural differences found in children's differing

moral consciousness in other countries and cultures. According to Cole (1964) in many societies, the culture of early childhood includes the skills and knowledge necessary to meet social as well as work obligations and responsibilities. Proper behavior in the presence of elders is often a prime obligation. In many societies adults are in charge and to them are owed both respect and obedience. These obligations are well understood and sharply etched among the patterns of childhood cultures.

However, in this particular study, 50 percent of the respondents of the parent questionnaire said if children did not respect the elderly it was not the fault of the parents. Many theorist also support some of these perceptions by indicating that preschool children operate at a global cognitive level of classification and, therefore, are not yet able to distinguish specifications to evaluate events, persons, or objects until they are developmentally ready. Is this in fact a culturally determined event and accepted fact or a universal occurrence, therefore a developmental theory? More cross cultural work is necessary.

Implication for Practical Use

The results from this study could be useful to parents and all other persons who are interested in children. It should provide teachers, school administrators, and curriculum developers with further information on which to base their decision about whether or not to include elderly volunteers and specific experiences as strategies for changing or influencing children's perceptions. For the child's interaction with others are only a part of a world or social order perceived by the child and as Dubin and Dubin comment: "...a child's behavior and attitudes do not seem to be closely related to any particular aspect of the home or early environment; they seem, rather, to be determined by the nature of the child and his relation to the total psychological field in which he functions...."

From the point of view of this researcher the "field" is the total environment - the ecosystem. The inherent biological make-up and the forces from the environment, together in complex interaction, affect the course of the developing individual but do not wholly determine it.

BIBLIOGRAPHY

Allport, G.W. "Attitudes." In A Handbook of Social Psychology, pp. 798-844. Edited by C.A. Murchison. Worcester, Mass.: Clark University Press, 1935.

_____. The Nature of Prejudice. Reading, Mass.: Addison-Wesley, 1954.

Anderson, C.M. "The Self Image: A Theory of the Dynamics of Behavior." In Readings in Child Adolescent Psychology, pp. 407-18. Edited by L.D. Crow and A. Crow. New York: Longmans, 1961.

Bandura, Albert, and Huston, Aletha. "Identification as a Process of Incidental Learning." In Readings in Psychology of Parent-Child Relations. Edited by Gene R. Medinnus. New York: John Wiley & Sons, Inc., 1967.

Bandura, Albert. Origins of Behavior, Social Learning Theory. Englewood Cliffs, N.J.: Prentice-Hall, Inc., 1977.

Bell, Richard Q., and Harper, Laurence V. Child Effects on Adults. Hillsdale, N.J.: Lawrence Erlbaum Associates, Publishers, 1977.

Campbell, Donald, and and Stanley, Julien. Experimental and Quasi-Experimental Design for Research. Chicago: Rand McNally College Publishing Co., 1963.

Cole, Robert. Children in Crisis. Boston: Little, Brown, and Co., 1964.

Cottrell, Fred. Aging and the Aged. Dubuque, Iowa: WM. C. Brown Co. Publishers, 1974.

Dickman, H.R. "The Perception of Behavioral Units." In The Stream of Behavior. Edited by R.B. Barker. New York: Appleton-Century-Crofts, 1963.

Dubin, R., and Dubin, E.R. "Children's Social Perceptions: A Review of Research." Child Development 36 (1965): 809-38.

Elkin, Frederick. _The Child and Society_. New York: Random House, 1960.

Emmerich, W. "Young Children's Discriminations of Parents and Child Roles." _Child Development_ 30 (1959): 403-19.

Emmerich, W.; Goldman, K.S.; and Shore, R.E. "Differentiation and Development of Social Norms." _Journal of Personality and Social Psychology_ 18 (1971): 323-53.

Erickson, E.H. "Identity and the Life Cycle." _Psychological Issues_ 1 (1969).

Erickson, H. _Identity Youth & Crisis_. New York: Norton, 1968.

Esterbrook, J.A. "The Effect of Emotion on Cue Utilization and the Organization of Behavior." _Psychological Review_ 66 (1959): 183-201.

Flapan, D. _Children's Understanding of Social Interaction_. New York: Teachers College Press, 1968.

Garrison, Karl C., and Jones, Franklin R. _The Psychology of Human Development_. Scranton, Penn.: International Textbook Co., 1969.

Gibson, Eleanor. _Principles of Perceptual Learning and Development_. New York: Meredith Corporation, 1969.

Golde, P., and Kogan, N. "A Sentence Completion Procedure for Assessing Attitude Toward Old People." _Journal of Gerontology_ 14 (1959): 355-63.

Gollin, E.S. "Organizational Characteristics of Social Judgments: A Developmental Investigation." _Journal of Personality_ 26 (1958): 139-54.

Goodman, Mary Ellen. _The Culture of Childhood_. Teachers College, Columbia University: Teachers College Press, 1970.

Hawkes, G.R. "The Child in the Family." _Marriage & Family Living_ 47 (1957).

Hawkes, G.R.; Burchinal, L.G.; and Gardner, B. "Preadoles-
     cents' Views of Some of Their Relations with Their
     Parents." Child Development 28 (1957): 393-99.

Hays, William. Statistics for the Social Sciences. New
     York: Holt, Rinehart and Winston, Inc., 1973.

Hess, R.D., and Torney, Judith. "Religion, Age and Sex in
     Children's Perceptions of Family Authority." Child
     Development 33 (1962): 781-89.

Hickey, Tom, and Kalish, Richard. "Young People's Perceptions
     of Adults." Journal of Gerontology 23 (April 1968):215-19.

Hill, Russell, and Stafford, Frank. "Allocation of Time to
     Preschool Children and Educational Opportunity." Pre-
     sented at the Econometric Society Meeting, New Orleans,
     Louisiana, December 1971 (revised February 1972).

Isaac, Stephen, and Michael, William. Handbook in Research
     and Evaluation. San Diego, Calif.: Edit's Publishers,
     1971.

Jantz, R.K.; Seefeldt, D.; Galper, A; and Serock, K. Child-
     ren's Attitudes toward the Elderly: Final Report.
     College Park, Md.: University of Maryland, 1976.

Jantz, Richard K.; Seefeldt, Carole; Galper, Alice; and Serock,
     Kathy. "Children's Attitudes toward the Elderly."
     Social Education, October 1977, pp. 518-23.

Johnson, Elizabeth, and Bursk, Barbara. "Relationships bet-
     ween the Elderly and Their Adult Children." The
     Gerontologist 17 (1977).

Kastenbaum, R., and Durke, N. "Young People View Old Age."
     In New Thoughts on Old Age, pp. 237-49. Edited by R.
     Kastenbaum. New York: Springer Publishing Co., 1964.

Kell, Leone, and Aldores, Joan. "The Relation between Mother's
     Childbearing Ideologies and Their Children's Perceptions
     of Maternal Control." Child Development 31 (1960):145-56.

Kephart, W.N. The Family, Society and the Individual.
     Boston: Houghton Mifflin, 1961.

Kerlinger, F.N. <u>Foundations of Behavioral Research</u>. New York: Holt, Rinehart and Winston, Inc., 1973.

Klausmeier, Herbert J. <u>Learning and Human Abilities</u>. New York: Harper and Row Publishers, 1971.

Klausmeier, H.J., and Goodwin, W. <u>Learning and Human Abilities Educational Psychology</u>. 2d ed. New York: Harper, 1966.

Kluckhohn, C. "Culture and Behavior." In <u>Handbook of Social Psychology</u>, Vol. I. Edited by G. Lindzey. Reading, Mass.: Addison, Wesley, 1954.

_____. <u>Culture and Behavior</u>. New York: Free Press of Glencoe, 1962.

Kohlberg, Lawrence. "Development of Moral Character and Moral Ideology." In <u>Review of Child Development Research</u>. Edited by M.C. Hoffman and L.W. Hoffman. New York: Russell Sage Foundation, 1964.

Kohn, A.R., and Fiedler, F.E. "Age and Sex Differences in the Perception of Persons." <u>Sociometry</u> 24 (1961):157-64.

Langer, J. "Werner's Comparative Organismic Theory." In <u>Carmichael's Manual of Child Psychology</u>, Vol. I. Edited by P.H. Mussen. New York: Wiley & Sons, 1970.

Laurence, J.H. "The Effect of Perceived Age on Initial Impressions and Normative Role Expectations." <u>International Journal of Aging and Human Development</u> 5 (1974): 369-91.

Livesley, W.J., and Bromley, D.B. <u>Person Perception in Childhood and Adolescence</u>. London: Wiley, 1973.

Logan, F.; Olmsted, D.L.; Rosner, B.S.; Schwartz, R.D.; and Stevens, C.M. <u>Behavior Theory and Social Science</u>. New Haven: Yale University Press, 1955.

Maccoby, Eleanor E., and Wilson, William C. "Identification and Observational Learning from Films." <u>The Journal of Abnormal and Social Psychology</u> 55 (1957): 76-86.

McTavish, D.G. "Perceptions of Old Age: A Review of Research Methodologies and Findings." Gerontologist 11 (1971): 90-101.

Meltzer, H. "Sex Differences in Children's Attitudes to Parents." Journal of Genetic Psychology 62 (1943): 311-26.

Merleau-Ponty. The Primacy of Perception. Edited by James M. Edie. Northwestern University Press, 1964.

Mussen, P.H.; Conger, J.J.; and Kagan, J. Child Development and Personality. New York: Harper and Row, Publishers, 1969.

Peevers, B.H., and Secord, P.F. "Developmental Changes in Attribution of Descriptive Concepts to Persons." Journal of Personality and Social Psychology 27 (1973): 120-28.

Piaget, Jean. Language and Thought of the Child. London: Routledge and Kegan Paul, 1932.

_____. The Origins of Intelligence in Children. New York: W.W. Norton & Co., Inc., 1952.

Pickering, Sir George. "Education for Tomorrow: A Biologist's View." In Lifelong Learning, pp. 1-13. Edited by F.W. Jessup. New York: Pergamon Press, 1969.

Proshansky, H., and Newton, P. "The Nature and Meaning of Negro Self-Identity." In Social Class, Race and Psychological Development, pp. 178-218. Edited by M. Deutsch, I. Katz, and A.R. Jensen. New York: Holt, Rinehart & Winston, 1968.

Rubin, Lillian. Worlds of Pain. New York: Basic Books, 1976.

Scarlett, H.H.; Press, A.N.; and Crockett, W.H. "Children's Description of Peers; A Wernerian Developmental Analysis." Child Development 42 (1971): 439-53.

Sears, R.R.; Maccoby, Eleanor E.; and Levin, H. Patterns of Child Rearing. Evanston, Ill.: Row Peterson, 1957.

Shantz, Carolyn Uhlinger. The Development of Social Cognition. Chicago: The University of Chicago Press, 1975.

Sigel, I.E.; Saltz, E.; and Roskind, W. "Variables Determining Concept Conservation in Children." Journal of Experimental Psychology 74 (1967): 471-75.

Signell, K.A. "Cognitive Complexity in Person Perception and Nation Perception: A Developmental Approach." Journal of Personality 34 (1966): 517-37.

Simmons, Katrina; Greenberg, Bradley; and Atkin, Charles. "The Demography of Fictional Television Characters in 1975-76." Department of Communication, Michigan State University, Castle Report Number Two. U.S. Office of Child Development, Washington, D.C.

Slater, Philip E. "Cultural Attitudes toward the Aged." Geriatrics 18 (April 1963): 308-14.

Solley, Charles M., and Murphy, G. Development of the Perceptual World. New York: Basic Books, Inc., 1960.

Thomas, E.C., and Yamamoto, K. "Attitudes toward Age: An Exploration in School Age Children." International Journal of Aging and Human Development 6 (1975): 117-25.

Treybig, D.C. "Language, Children and Attitudes toward the Aged." Gerontologist 14 (1974): 14-75.

Tukman, J., and Lorge, I. "Perceptual Stereotypes about Life Adjustment." Journal of Social Psychology 43 (1956): 239-45.

Werner, H. Comparative Psychology of Mental Development. New York: International University Press, 1948.

Wetters, Doris. "Creative Aspects of Home Manager's Resourcefulness." Ed.D. dissertation, Pennsylvania State University, 1967.

Yarrow, Marian. "The Measurement of Children's Attitudes and Values." In Handbook of Research Methods in Child Development, pp. 645-87. Edited by P.H. Mussen. New York: Wiley, 1960.

Yarrow, M.R., and Campbell, J.D. "Person Perception in Children." <u>Merrill-Palmer Quarterly</u> 9 (1963): 57-72.

OTHER TITLES AVAILABLE FROM
CENTURY TWENTY ONE PUBLISHING

NEW DIRECTIONS IN ETHNIC STUDIES: MINORITIES IN AMERICA by David
    Claerbaut, Editor   Perfect Bound   LC# 80-69327
    ISBN 0-86548-025-7 $9.95
COLLECTING, CULTURING, AND CARING FOR LIVING MATERIALS: GUIDE FOR
    TEACHER, STUDENT AND HOBBYIST by William E. Claflin   Perfect
    Bound   LC# 80-69329   ISBN 0-86548-026-5 $8.50
TEACHING ABOUT THE OTHER AMERICANS: MINORITIES IN UNITED STATES
    HISTORY by Ann Curry   Perfect Bound   LC# 80-69120
    ISBN 0-86548-028-1 $8.95
MULTICULTURAL TRANSACTIONS: A WORKBOOK FOCUSING ON COMMUNICATION
    BETWEEN GROUPS by James S. DeLo and William A. Green   Perfect
    Bound   LC# 80-69328   ISBN 0-86548-030-3 $11.50
LEARNING TO TEACH by Richard B. Dierenfield   Perfect Bound
    LC# 80-69119   ISBN 0-86548-031-1 $10.95
LEARNING TO THINK--TO LEARN by M. Ann Dirkes   Perfect Bound
    LC# 80-65613   ISBN 0-86548-032-X $11.50
PLAY IN PRESCHOOL MAINSTREAMED AND HANDICAPPED SETTINGS by Anne Cairns
    Federlein   Perfect Bound   LC# 80-65612   ISBN 0-86548-035-4
    $10.50
THE NATURE OF LEADERSHIP FOR HISPANICS AND OTHER MINORITIES by
    Ernest Yutze Flores   Perfect Bound   LC# 80-69239
    ISBN 0-86548-036-2 $10.95
THE MINI-GUIDE TO LEADERSHIP by Ernest Yutze Flores   Perfect Bound
    LC# 80-83627   ISBN 0-86548-037-0 $5.50
THOUGHTS, TROUBLES AND THINGS ABOUT READING FROM THE CRADLE THROUGH
    GRADE THREE by Carolyn T. Gracenin   Perfect Bound
    LC# 80-65611   ISBN 0-86548-038-9 $14.95
BETWEEN TWO CULTURES: THE VIETNAMESE IN AMERICA by Alan B. Henkin and
    Liem Thanh Nguyen   Perfect Bound   LC# 80-69333
    ISBN 0-86548-039-7 $7.95
PERSONALITY CHARACTERISTICS AND DISCIPLINARY ATTITUDES OF CHILD-
    ABUSING MOTHERS by Alan L. Evans   Perfect Bound   LC# 80-69240
    ISBN 0-86548-033-8 $11.95
PARENTAL EXPECTATIONS AND ATTITUDES ABOUT CHILDREARING IN HIGH RISK
    VS. LOW RISK CHILD ABUSING FAMILIES by Gary C. Rosenblatt
    Perfect Bound   LC# 79-93294   ISBN 0-86548-020-6 $10.00
CHILD ABUSE AS VIEWED BY SUBURBAN ELEMENTARY SCHOOL TEACHERS by David
    A. Pelcovitz   Perfect Bound   LC# 79-93295   ISBN 0-86548-019-2
    $10.00
PHYSICAL CHILD ABUSE: AN EXPANDED ANALYSIS by James R. Seaberg
    Perfect Bound   LC# 79-93293   ISBN 0-86548-021-4 $10.00
THE DISPOSITION OF REPORTED CHILD ABUSE by Marc F. Maden   Perfect
    Bound   LC# 79-93296   ISBN 0-86548-016-8 $10.00
EDUCATIONAL AND PSYCHOLOGICAL PROBLEMS OF ABUSED CHILDREN by James
    Christiansen   Perfect Bound   LC# 79-93303   ISBN 0-86548-003-6
    $10.00
DEPENDENCY, FRUSTRATION TOLERANCE, AND IMPULSE CONTROL IN CHILD ABUSERS
    by Don Kertzman   Perfect Bound   LC# 79-93297   ISBN 86548-015-X
    $10.00
SUCCESSFUL STUDENT TEACHING: A HANDBOOK FOR ELEMENTARY AND SECONDARY
    STUDENT TEACHERS by Fillmer Hevener, Jr.   Perfect Bound
    LC# 80-69332   ISBN 0-86548-040-0 $8.95
BLACK COMMUNICATION IN WHITE SOCIETY by Roy Cogdell and Sybil Wilson
    Perfect Bound   LC# 79-93302   ISBN 0-86548-004-4 $13.00

SCHOOL VANDALISM: CAUSE AND CURE by Robert Bruce Williams and Joseph
    L. Venturini   Perfect Bound   LC# 80-69230   ISBN 0-86548-060-5
    $9.50
LEADERS, LEADING, AND LEADERSHIP by Harold W. Boles   Perfect Bound
    LC# 80-65616   ISBN 0-86548-023-0 $14.95
LEGAL OUTLOOK: A MESSAGE TO COLLEGE AND UNIVERSITY PEOPLE by Ulysses
    V. Spiva Perfect Bound   LC# 80-69232   ISBN 0-86548-057-5
    $9.95
THE NAKED CHILD THE LONG RANGE EFFECTS OF FAMILY AND SOCIAL NUDITY
    by Dennis Craig Smith Perfect Bound   LC# 80-69234
    ISBN 0-86548-056-7 $7.95
SIGNIFICANT INFLUENCE PEOPLE: A SIP OF DISCIPLINE AND ENCOURAGEMENT
    by Joseph C. Rotter, Johnnie McFadden and Gary D. Kannenberg
    Perfect Bound   LC# 80-69233   ISBN 0-86548-055-9 $8.95
LET'S HAVE FUN WITH ENGLISH by Ruth Rackmill   Perfect Bound
    LC# 80-68407   ISBN 0-86548-061-3 $6.95
CHILDREN'S PERCEPTIONS OF ELDERLY PERSONS by Lillian A. Phenice
    Perfect Bound   LC# 80-65604   ISBN 0-86548-054-0 $10.50
URBAN EDUCATION: AN ANNOTATED BIBLIOGRAPHY by Arnold G. Parks
    Perfect Bound   LC# 80-69234   ISBN 0-86548-053-2 $9.50
DYNAMICS OF CLASSROOM STRUCTURE by Charles J. Nier   Perfect Bound
    LC# 80-69330   ISBN 0-86548-052-4 $11.50
SOCIOLOGY IN BONDAGE: AN INTRODUCTION TO GRADUATE STUDY by Harold A.
    Nelson   Perfect Bound   LC# 80-65605   ISBN 0-86548-051-6 $9.95
BEYOND THE OPEN CLASSROOM: TOWARD INFORMAL EDUCATION by Lorraine L.
    Morgan, Vivien C. Richman and Ann Baldwin Taylor   Perfect Bound
    LC# 80-69235   ISBN 0-86548-050-8 $9.50
INTRODUCTORY SOCIOLOGY: LECTURES, READINGS AND EXERCISES by Gordon D.
    Morgan   Perfect Bound   LC# 80-65606   ISBN 0-86548-049-4
    $10.50
THE STUDENT TEACHER ON THE FIRING LINE by D. Eugene Meyer   Perfect
    Bound   LC# 80-69236   ISBN 0-86548-048-6 $11.95
VALUES ORIENTATION IN SCHOOL by Johnnie McFadden and Joseph C. Rotter
    Perfect Bound   LC# 80-69238   ISBN 0-86548-045-1 $4.50
MOVEMENT THEMES: TOPICS FOR EARLY CHILDHOOD LEARNING THROUGH CREATIVE
    MOVEMENT by Barbara Stewart Jones   Perfect Bound   LC# 80-65608
    ISBN 0-86548-042-7 $8.50
FROM BIRTH TO TWELVE: HOW TO BE A SUCCESSFUL PARENT TO INFANTS AND
    CHILDREN by Gary D. Kannenberg   Perfect Bound   LC# 80-69331
    ISBN 0-86548-043-5 $7.95